WOMAN
OF LABRADOR

Elizabeth Goudie

edited and with an introduction
by David Zimmerly

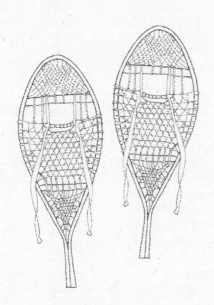

NIMBUS
PUBLISHING LTD

Nimbus Publishing Limited
PO Box 9166
Halifax, NS B3K 5M8
(902) 455-4286
www.nimbus.ca

David Zimmerly photos pp. 143 (bottom), 151 (bottom), 154, 155, 156, 157.
Cover design: Arthur B. Carter, Halifax
Printed and bound in Canada

Nimbus Publishing is committed to protecting our natural environment. As part of our efforts, this book is printed on 100% recycled content stock.

Library and Archives Canada Cataloguing in Publication Data
        Goudie, Elizabeth, 1902–1982.
        Woman of Labrador
        Includes bibliographical references.
        ISBN 1-55109-143-7
        ISBN 978-1-55109-143-3

1. Goudie, Elizabeth, 1902–1982. 2. Frontier and pioneer life—Newfoundland—Labrador. 3. Labrador (Nfld.)—Biography.

FC2193.3.G68 A3 1996   971.8'202'092   C96-950057-2
F1137.G68 19961

CONTENTS

INTRODUCTION

The life of the Labrador trapper, as seen from the man's point of view, is glorified in the writings of Elliot Merrick. In his 1933 book, *True North*, Merrick talks about the men he travelled and hunted with on their annual trek up the Hamilton River to their fur paths. We see the dashing waters, feel the numbing cold and hear the trappers' gripping tales. We hear the then and still now common names of the hardy Scotch, English and French trappers: the Blakes, Michelins, Montagues, Chaulks and Goudies. And among these yarns there is one about a woman who was *that* close to being attacked by a mad lynx. Her name was Elizabeth Goudie.

The lynx story, an incident out of the twenties, is still vividly remembered in every detail by Mrs. Goudie who is now in her seventies. She was pregnant then and the leaping animal gave her such a scare that she ... but that is for Mrs. Goudie to tell. This is her book, about her life in particular, but through her we can picture what and how all the trappers' wives lived. Not only is this the first book written about the Labrador woman, it is also the first written by a native-born Labrador woman.

Following the death of her husband in 1963, Mrs. Goudie found time going slowly and looking out the window at all the irreversible change that had taken place since

1940, she started to relive her past life—only in her mind at first—but then when she realized that her grandchildren could never know that other life, she decided to commit the events of her life to pen and paper. Armed with pencils, school scribblers, a fourth grade education and a lifetime of experiences, Mrs. Goudie has written a human document full of joy, fear, humour and tribulation.

Happy Valley, Labrador, the present home of Elizabeth Goudie, was only a sandy plain when she was born. It lies at the head of Hamilton Inlet where the Churchill, Goose and North West rivers debouch into Lake Melville. Also living in this area are several thousand American Air Force personnel and dependents who reside in typical American splendour and relative luxury in a compound known as Goose Air Base. Across the runway at Goose Bay live 3,000 mainland Canadians employed by the Royal Canadian Armed Forces, the Department of Transport and related service industries. The 5,000 inhabitants of Happy Valley are mostly European-descended Labradorians and island Newfoundlanders, but include a scattering of Montagnais/ Naskapi Indians, Labrador Eskimos and representatives of some thirty other nationalities. Eight miles downstream and across the river from Happy Valley is the community of Mud Lake whose 125 settlers commute daily by boat or snowmobile to jobs at Goose Air Base. Twenty-five miles northeast of Goose Bay is North West River, a divided community of 450 Montagnais/Naskapi Indians on one side of the river and 500 white settlers and a few Eskimos on the other side.

Human occupation of coastal and interior Labrador goes back almost 5,000 years to the Indian Maritime Archaic Tradition. Eskimos appeared about 800 B.C., disappeared only 600 years later and reappeared in the late 1500s. Although Labrador was one of the first parts of North America visited by Europeans in the tenth century and saw the passing of exploration ships of many nations during the fifteenth, sixteenth and seventeenth centuries, it remained for the Seigneur de Courtemanche to establish the first settlement in the early 1700s.

The French, in the person of Louis Fornel, are credited with the first year-round trading post within Hamilton Inlet in 1743 at the location of the present North West River. With the English takeover of Labrador in 1763, settlement was strictly discouraged in an attempt to preserve the salmon and codfishing grounds for English vessels and also on account of bad relations with the Eskimos who made settlement a precarious and dangerous proposition.

With the northward retreat of the Eskimos and the Moravian establishment of missions after 1770, this problem was somewhat alleviated and Captain Cartwright started furring and fishing enterprises just south of Hamilton Inlet in 1775. His dealings with the Eskimos, enlightened for the times, created a climate for friendly relations and English settlement in Hamilton Inlet commenced about 1785 with the arrival of William Phippard and John Nooks or Newhook. Out of necessity they took Eskimo women as wives and started the first settler families in Hamilton Inlet. They were followed by other settlers, Englishmen mostly, who found the prospects of life in Labrador more enticing than the possibility of being impressed on an English man-of-war. Some were merely adventurous and wanted only to make a life in an unknown land unfettered by laws or government. Mrs. Goudie's great-great-grandfather Ambrose Brooks was one of these Englishmen.

This first phase of settlement in Hamilton Inlet lasted from 1775 to 1835 and was the beginning stage for a way of life that endured almost to the middle of the twentieth century.

The technology available to the settlers came partially from their old European skills, but included borrowed traits that came from both the Indians and the Eskimos. Imbued with a Protestant work ethic, the early settlers were eager to tap all possible resources and were not encumbered with a previous culture history tying them down to either a maritime or inland niche such as were the Eskimos and Indians. The settlers Eskimo wives already had all the necessary skills for a coastal existence; from their talented hands came all the warm clothing used in the winter as well as the waterproof items such as sealskin boots used in the spring and summer. These skills and implements such as the *ulu* or crescent-shaped Eskimo woman's knife and its use in scraping seal skins, the *kamutik* (Eskimo dog-sled), the harpoon for taking seals at their breathing holes on the ice and the tailored pullover fur-trimmed Eskimo parka (called *dickie* by the settlers)—all these and more have survived to the present day even though the custom of taking Eskimo wives was discontinued over a hundred years ago. This latter was due in part to the dwindling number of available Eskimo women, but this in turn may have been caused by disease, northern migration and the debilitating effects of alcohol. Despite the fact that this could have been a real source of friction between the Eskimo men and the settlers, there are few recorded instances of trouble between them.

From the Montagnais/Naskapi Indians, the settlers learned the skills of trapping and survival in interior Labrador and borrowed many material items such as the toboggan, canoe, snowshoes and crooked knife. From their European background and knowledge, the settlers made log cabins for their families, log huts called *tilts* for use on their trap lines, homemade metal stoves for heat and cooking, wooden whaleboats for trips to their summer houses and numerous other items.

During the winter months when the men were out on the trapline, their wives were kept busy sewing clothes, chopping firewood, taking care of the children and other chores.

From the scattered information available for the early period, it is possible to abstract a very generalized picture of the yearly activities in the settlers' life. Starting in September, equipment and supplies were readied for the winter trapping. While the women made parkas, boots, mitts, etc., the men cut enough turns of wood (ten to twelve foot lengths of trees) to last their families through the winter months. By October the fur was prime enough for trapping and the men set out traplines that might hold up to 200 or 300 traps.

Dogs were not used on the trapline because of the deep, soft snow that rendered them useless. The trapper had to carry everything on his back or haul it on a toboggan. On his daily walk from one tilt to the next, he carried only a game and bait bag plus his knife, an axe and a few other essentials. At the end of the day he cut a supply of firewood, ate his supper consisting of unleavened bread and beans cooked the previous day, skinned and cleaned his catch, prepared bread and beans for the next day and then relied on the warmth of the stove alone to keep himself from freezing in the below-zero temperatures of the Labrador hinterlands.

This pace continued, with perhaps the alternation of a few caribou hunts, until spring when the men went out on frozen Lake Melville to shoot seals that came up on the ice to sun themselves. Ducks and geese returning from the south were also added to the larder at this time of year.

July was the month for catching salmon which ran up most of the streams draining into Lake Melville. Codfish, taken in August, were split, salted and dried for preservation. The settlers probably kept some of the salmon and cod for themselves but sold as much as possible to the merchants in order to buy their winter staples. Summer and early fall was also the time to make canoes, cut wood and gather berries. This lifestyle with seasonal movement between a summer coastal fishing house and the inland winter trapping quarters was an extremely rugged and lonely life for the settlers. Mrs. Goudie's great-grandmother, as a young girl in this period, reported that the closest people to her family were over seventy miles away.

In 1824, the Wesleyan Methodists sent a missionary to Hamilton Inlet charged with attending to the needs of the settlers and reporting on the advisability of establishing a mission in Labrador. A mission was not established. The Newfoundland government also set up provisions for a Circuit and Sessions Court that made yearly trips from 1826 to 1833 and was then abandoned because of lack of business and high cost of operation.

With the arrival in 1836 of the Hudson's Bay Company in Hamilton Inlet, a new wave of immigration was felt. Two main posts were established, one at North West River and the other at Rigolet. Competing traders in the area were soon bought out and the Hudson's Bay Company was able to enjoy a virtual trade monopoly for the next sixty years. The company's employees, mostly from England and Scotland, stayed for the five-year duration of their contracts and then either signed on for another term or returned to Britain or stayed on in Hamilton Inlet as independent settlers.

The company's emphasis on furs and their willingness to outfit a trapper who then worked on a "share" system, led many of the settlers to devote more time to trapping. They blazed their traplines further inland than before and made them longer, requiring that they stay on the fur-paths at least three full months.

From 1848 to the late 1860s the progressive Hudson's Bay Company Trader Donald A. Smith (he later became Lord Strathcona and Mount Royal) established policies that expanded the number of posts under him, showed good profits for the Company and proved the feasibility of raising vegetables and livestock in North West River. Through his example the settlers also began raising crops of potatoes and turnips although on a less systematic basis.

In 1854 Smith visited the Moravians on the north coast attempting to induce them to establish a mission in Hamilton Inlet. A return visit by the Moravian missionary Brother Elsner in 1857 was appreciated, but the mission was not established.

The Labrador Circuit Court, abandoned in 1833, was re-established in 1863 and ran until 1874. The duties of the judges chiefly consisted of the proper discharge of the law, but they were also called upon to take the census, pay school teachers, distribute school books and dispense medicines and relief. Legal cases most often encountered included debt, trespass, disturbing the peace, theft, assault and battery, and bastardy, in that order of occurrence. The total case load was very light and only the more severe ones were handled by the Circuit Court. During the rest of the year, minor problems were settled by appointed Justices of the Peace, usually an official of the Hudson's

Bay Company. The latter were often empowered to perform marriages and they provided other services normally in the province of the clergy.

The Moravians made another attempt to investigate the possibilities of a mission in Hamilton Inlet in 1873. Again, the outcome was against establishment.

In 1883 the Wesleyan Methodists established a permanent mission in Hamilton Inlet near Rigolet, followed several years later by a mission teacher. Both teacher and minister went to the people, visiting every family at least once during the year, either by dogteam or boat.

The first tourist attempt to see the Grand (Churchill) Falls was in 1887. The ensuing published article on this attempt stimulated interest in the area among adventurers and scientists alike. The Geological Survey of Canada conducted a major exploration of inland Labrador in 1893–94 headed by A. P. Low. Spending a good part of the fall and winter in North West River, Low made important observations on the geology of the area.

Between 1901 and 1941 the trapping lifestyle was intensified but a number of historical events were responsible for changes in the culture that heralded the eventual downfall of the trapping way of life.

In 1901 the Revillon Frères Trading Company established a post in North West River, breaking the virtual trade monopoly held by the Hudson's Bay Company for over sixty years. The result was better fur prices for the trappers.

By 1904 there was a full-scale lumbering operation in Mud Lake and Carter Basin that attracted a number of settlers from various regions of Labrador. Most of the workers were from Nova Scotia and Newfoundland. When the operations collapsed after little more than ten years, most of the men went back home; a few local women married lumbermen and left with them. For the settlers this was the first taste of wage-labour work. The timber grants issued by the Newfoundland Government also precipitated the Labrador Boundary Dispute with Quebec. This was settled in Newfoundland's favour in 1927.

Expeditions by adventurers in 1903 and 1905 saw the death of one man from starvation and exposure. The man had been editor for *Outing* magazine in the United States and his death focussed wide attention on the North West River area of Labrador. Books by other members of the expeditions were widely read and garnered much sympathy for Hubbard, the man who perished, and for the people of Hamilton Inlet. This may have contributed to the fund-raising success of the next group to enter the Labrador scene.

After a number of medical and missionary-type trips to the coast of Labrador by Wilfred T. Grenfell, an organization was born known as the International Grenfell Association. Their stated charter or mission was to care for the complete welfare of Labrador people and the summer fishermen from Newfoundland who inhabited its coast. This included medical, educational, spiritual and physical aid administered through several hospitals and boarding schools. Responsibility for health and education had previously been left to the settlers.

The health care improved in 1912 when a year-round hospital was started in Mud Lake and full-time education became available in 1926 when a boarding school was built in North West River.

The First World War decreased the isolation of many settlers with some joining the Newfoundland Regiment to fight abroad while others raised money for the war effort.

A few of these men were killed in Europe but the largest death toll among the settlers occurred in 1918 when returning soldiers brought an influenza epidemic with them that killed close to a quarter of the population.

In 1934 the Newfoundland Government fell from its Dominion status and was administered by a British Commission of Government. One result for Labrador was the stationing of a number of outposts of Newfoundland Rangers, a rural police force. While their duties and powers were relatively small, they were another outside force bringing new ideas. The depression of the 1930s also affected the settlers who had to accept less money for their furs due to a decreased world demand for them.

With the start of World War II, a massive effort was mounted to develop a system of air bases to ferry men and materials from North America to Europe. Goose Bay was chosen in 1941 as one of these sites and in a short time the area was inundated with construction personnel and equipment sufficient to build a large modern airport and a city for 8,000 people.

As most eligible Canadians were already either in the armed services or otherwise engaged in the war effort, construction labour was at a premium. Jobs were available and waiting for willing men of almost any skill or lack of it. Labrador's settlers had already been hurt by the falling prices for their fish and furs and jumped at the chance to have steady employment at wages higher than any had ever heard of. They came to Goose Bay from all parts of Labrador; some came alone, some with families, dogs and baggage. They arrived by dog team, rowboat, canoe, motorboat—even by foot on snowshoes.

Pitching their tents and log tilts first on Otter Creek near the new base, the settlers were soon ordered to move to an area no closer than five miles from the military reserve. They chose a spot on the Hamilton (Churchill) River, erected tents in small clearings they hacked out of the thick bush and within two or three weeks had managed to build small houses that were barely sufficient for their families' needs.

Variously called Skunk Hollow, Hamilton River Village and finally Happy Valley, the frontier town's population slowly grew to more than 600 people by the end of 1951. By this time the Cold War had started and American activity on the base increased as construction of radar warning sites took place in the Arctic. The facilities at Goose Air Base were being continually expanded and updated, creating a demand for labour that Labrador could not alone supply. Happy Valley had been composed almost entirely of native Labradorians, but now experienced a wave of immigrants who came mostly from Newfoundland and who by 1956 almost outnumbered the Labradorians.

Between 1956 and 1972, Happy Valley slowly acquired churches, schools, stores, telephones, electricity, hotel, taxi service, a bank, water and sewage systems and became incorporated as a town with an elected Town Council. Meanwhile, the interior of Labrador was being developed by Newfoundland Premier Joseph Smallwood through complicated manoeuvring and uniting with a number of unsavoury promoters. The result was the formation of two new modern mining towns, Wabush and Labrador City and a hydro-electric project at Grand (Churchill) Falls with a power potential of 7 million horsepower. While a few residents left Happy Valley to work on these new developments, most Labradorians lacked the technical skills necessary for continued employment in the mines or at the dam.

The latest development to affect Happy Valley occurred in 1969 when Canadian Javelin started logging operations in the area to supply pulpwood for a new linerboard mill at Stephenville in western Newfoundland. These activities coincided with a phase-down of operations on the American base and helped stall economic collapse in the area. After the fall of the Smallwood regime in 1971, the new Tory government in Newfoundland took over operation of the logging industry as well as the linerboard mill in Stephenville, preventing collapse. The American evacuation of Goose Air Base is proceeding rapidly, with the job void thus created being taken over by the Ministry of Transport. This ever quickening rate of change in the Goose Bay area makes it extremely difficult to predict the future even ten years from now. Residents of Happy Valley can themselves barely believe the changes that have occurred in their part of the world.

The communities so familiar to Mrs. Goudie in the pre-World War II years are only memories now, their inhabitants having long since moved to Happy Valley or North West River. These places—Mulligan, Pearl River, Sebaskachu, Kenemich and others—still live in the minds of the older people of Happy Valley and now through the writings of Mrs. Goudie. Her life has spanned two different cultures.

From 1900 to 1940 the changes and improvements in life came slowly—a resident minister, doctors and a hospital, schools, radio communications; important additions for the people of Labrador. Mrs. Goudie remembers when they came and tells of their impact.

She has also seen firsthand the changes and developments since World War II including the Churchill Falls hydro-electric project, which now straddles land her husband and relatives once trapped. Being immensely proud of her land of Labrador, Elizabeth Goudie has few good words for those who would drain off the mighty woods and water resources at the expense of the people of Labrador. For ex-Premier Joe Smallwood it was a dream come true to arbitrarily change the name of Hamilton River to Churchill River, to dam up the lakes and streams and reduce the once magnificent Grand Falls to a trickle and to sell off the luxuriant spruce forests to outside tree miners, but to Elizabeth Goudie it was sacrilege pure and simple. This was her land, her husband's land, the land of her ancestors and never once was she or any other Labradorian consulted. The alteration of the face of Labrador was entirely outside their sphere of influence.

All this has not made Mrs. Goudie bitter, only sad. The price of electricity, running water, indoor toilets and steady wage employment was not cheap—it cost the freedom, the independence, the self-sufficiency of the Labrador people. Mrs. Goudie is of the last generation of real pioneers. Her fierce and stubborn refusal to give up, to be licked, must draw upon some secret inner strengths and forces that have become extinct in most of mankind. At seventy years of age she still maintains her home single-handedly, takes in boarders to meet expenses rather than succumb to welfare, is still the closest thing to the ideal Christian and is able to enjoy life now as well as to look forward and backward. She has probably suffered through more personal physical and emotional pain during her life than most people would in a dozen lifetimes, but she remains cheerful, full of old yarns and ready to meet head-on with anything.

I met Mrs. Goudie during the year my family and I spent living in Happy Valley where I was doing anthropological research for Memorial University of Newfoundland.

I heard of her writing project and went to see her about it. After I learned that she had no one to edit and process her manuscript I volunteered to do it and make arrangements for publication. We spent many sessions in her kitchen working over the manuscript, always well fortified with her never-ending supply of tea and redberry pie. It is with affection and honour that I introduce the book of Elizabeth Goudie.

David W. Zimmerly
Ottawa, July 1973

SUGGESTED READING

Ayling, Vera. "The Goose Bay Story." *The Atlantic Advocate*, 54(10), pp. 27–30. Fredericton: 1964.

Burden, A. D. "The Glory of the Goose." *Dateline Labrador*, 1(4), pp. 10, 11, 13–16, 19–23, 25, 26. 1965.

Carr, W. G. *Checkmate in the North*. Toronto: 1944.

Cooke, Alan. "The Grand Falls." *Beaver*, Outfit 289, Winter, pp. 34–38. Winnipeg: 1958.

———. "A Woman's Way." *Beaver*, Outfit 291, Summer, pp. 40–45. Winnipeg: 1960.

Davies, W. H. A. "Notes on Esquimaux Bay and the Surrounding Country." *Transactions*, 4(l), pp. 70–94. Literary and Historical Society of Quebec. Quebec: 1843.

Findlay, David K. "Goose: Key Air Base." *Maclean's Magazine*, June 15, pp. 12, 13, 42, 47. Toronto: 1943.

Fitzhugh, William W. "Environmental Archeology and Cultural Systems in Hamilton Inlet, Labrador." *Smithsonian Contributions to Anthropology*, Number 16. Washington: 1972.

Gosling, W. G. *Labrador: Its Discovery, Exploration, and Development*. London: 1910.

Grenfell, Wilfred T. et al. *Labrador: The Country and the People*. New York: 1910.

Hallock, Charles. "Three Months in Labrador." *Harper's New Monthly*, 22(81), pp. 577–99, 743–765. 1861.

Hubbard, Mrs. Leonidas, Junior. A *Woman's Way Through Unknown Labrador*. New York: 1908.

LeBourdais, D. M. "North West River." *Beaver*, Outfit 293, Spring, pp. 14–21. Winnipeg: 1963.

Merrick, Elliott. *True North*. New York: 1933.

———. *Northern Nurse*. New York: 1944.

Pickett, P. H. "Goose Airport: Gateway of the North." *Atlantic Guardian*, 4(3), pp. 16–20. 1947.

Scott J. M. *The Land that God Gave Cain: An Account of H. G. Watkin's Expedition to Labrador, 1928–1929.* London: 1933.

Tanner, V. *Outlines of the Geography, Life and Customs of Newfoundland-Labrador.* Cambridge: 1947.

Wallace, Dillon. *The Long Labrador Trail.* London: 1907.

———. *The Lure of the Labrador Wild.* Toronto: 1915.

Wright, Kenneth. "How Goose Bay Was Discovered." *Beaver,* Outfit 277, June, pp. 42–45. Winnipeg: 1946.

Young, Arminius. *A Methodist Missionary in Labrador.* Toronto: 1916.

———. *One Hundred Years of Mission Work in the Wilds of Labrador.* London:1931.

Zimmerly, David W. *Cain's Land Revisited: Culture Change in Central Labrador, 1775–1972.* Unpublished Ph.D. dissertation, University of Colorado. pp. 345. 1973. (In Press, Institute of Social and Economic Research, Memorial University of Newfoundland, St. John's, Nfld.)

I
THE LIFE OF A LABRADOR GIRL

In my dreams I'll go back to when I was a lad,
to the old country home; there was Mother and
*   my Dad,*
such kind, friendly neighbours make you think
*   you're their own.*
I'll keep dreaming of you, my riverside home.

—adapted from a song by John Chaulk

1. Family History

In approximately the year 1806, our great-great-grand-mother, who was an Eskimo orphan, ran away from down Rigolet Eskimos. The Eskimos there thought she had an evil spirit because her family died and they were going to cut her finger and bleed the bad blood out. She was afraid and ran away and came up (west) on the north side of Hamilton Inlet. There were no people living between Rigolet and North West River then, but a man named Brooks was tending his salmon nets on Pearl River, about twenty miles from North West River, and he saw her off in the distance. He went and picked her up. She could not speak English so he took her to North West River and got another Eskimo who spoke English to talk to her.

She lived with a family in North West River and later Brooks married her, but not until he taught her enough English to say the Lord's Prayer. When he married her she was between fourteen and fifteen years old.

As far as I know, Brooks only had two daughters by her. One, Lydia, was the mother of the Campbells and the other, Hannah, was the mother of the Michelins. Hannah married Mersai Michella[1] who was a French-Canadian trapper from Three Rivers, Quebec. He came out here as a servant for the Hudson's Bay Company. They settled in a place called Sebaskachu, about eighteen miles from

North West River. Hannah was my great-grandmother on my mother's side.

Mersai and Sarah had a son, John, who married Elizabeth Oliver and they had a daughter, Sarah, who married Joseph Blake. Joseph's father was Mark Blake, a Hudson's Bay Company servant at North West River who came from England. Sarah and Joseph Blake were my parents. I married in the Goudie family and there the family got Indian blood. John Goudie, my husband's grandfather, went up Hudson Bay and got his wife. She was half Cree and half Scot. John Goudie was a Scotsman so our family have quite a mixture—Eskimo, English, French, Scottish and Indian. My children are proud of their Indian and Scotch blood.

First I would like to make a note of my father and mother's life as they told it to me. My father was left without a father at the age of fifteen. He also had four sisters left with him so this meant he had to start out and learn to be a trapper. He was expected to help maintain them. At that time he lived down in Rigolet. He came up the Hamilton Inlet and up the Hamilton River and built a trapping place which was called Slack Waters. Now the Hamilton Inlet was called at that time Groswater Bay. I can remember well when all the Labrador folks called it Groswater Bay.

My mother's name was Sarah Michelin. She was left without a mother at the age of two years. Her mother died, she told us, of childbirth. Later her father married again. She lived with her step-mother until she was fourteen. Then she went with the Hudson's Bay Manager's sister as a servant girl at North West River. Their name was Cotter. The sister's name was Agnes Cotter. My mother stayed there then until she was twenty-four years old when she married my father, Joseph Blake. My father died in 1957 at age eighty-two. My mother Sarah was born in 1877 and she died in 1956.

My father's grandfather came out from England also as a servant for the Hudson's Bay Company. So the Hamilton Inlet was populated by the white people who came out here from Scotland, England and Canada, so we were told. They married among the Eskimo and Indian people. According to my parents this happened about two hundred years ago.

My grandfather Blake was counted to be one of the smartest runners in Groswater Bay. At that time, we were told, he could run down a caribou on the hard snow and shoot it. My father told me it was the cause of his death. He was running after caribou and one of the other trappers found him down on the snow and he died shortly after. This little note was handed down from our forefathers.

2. Childhood Memories

I was born April 20, 1902, at Mud Lake, Labrador. I was the oldest and my father kind of took me over and saw to it I did my share of the work. Mother was always busy with the smaller ones so I had to do girls' work and boys' work too. Father was often around when I was doing my work and saw to it I did it right, so I spent a lot of time with him and he became one of the best friends of my life besides being my father. He was a gentle man and he was kind but we didn't get away with anything. When we were told to do something we had to do it without any delay, but I always respected him for that.

I remember so well when my father started expecting me to get out of bed at five o'clock in the morning and have my mother's breakfast on the table by six o'clock. To me it seemed to be a very hard task, but I made a try at it. This was the beginning of a hard working life for me and this was expected of the average Labrador girl at that time.

Father's work

In 1907 there was a lumber company stationed in Mud Lake that came in from Nova Scotia. It was called the Dickey Lumber Company. My father worked with them on the log drives. That was his job. The logging was done by manpower and horses. There were quite a number of horses. I can remember that well because I was very afraid of them. They also brought in cows, pigs and sheep.

Schooling

Mud Lake was quite a place in 1907. There were a number of families who came in from Canada[2] and a number of people who moved in from along the shores of the Hamilton Inlet. They decided to build a church-school there. What I mean is that it was used for both church services and school purposes. I started going there when I was five years old. I remember the beginner's book was called the Primer. We often called it Tom's Dog Book because on the cover of the book there was a dog.

One of the local young ladies finished her school in Mud Lake, went to St. John's, Newfoundland, to college and later came back and went teaching along the shores of the Hamilton Inlet. Her name was Esther Best, a Labrador girl. This was the first teacher we had in this part of Labrador at that time—a Labrador-born girl. A little later another Labrador girl became a teacher also. Her name was May Baikie.

There were five villages along the shores as far out as Pearl River. The average size of a village was from three to five families. The two teachers on an average travelled about sixty miles by dog team. They spent about two and a half months at a place. I had the privilege of going to school two winters.

I spent three years in school in Mud Lake but really I had about four years in school if it were all put together. I got as far as the fourth grade in the old English readers and the Kirkland Scott Arithmetic Book. So I did not get very much education by books. But there was always something interesting in life. I always enjoyed life along the way.

First job

As I grew older the war came and I had to go out and earn my own bread, so to speak. I never was home very much after the age of fourteen. The wages were very low. I went to work for two dollars a month. If the family was very poor you only got your food or maybe the makings of a new dress. This work wasn't easy. You had to do everything by hand: scrub, wash, bring wood and water, help to cook and mend clothing. We never had a dull moment. Life in Labrador was a life of hard work, but we had peace of mind and contented hearts, and I think this was what made life worthwhile.

Spiritual life

One of the things our parents were concerned about was our spiritual life. The Bible was read daily in the homes. That was the last thing that was done at night. Sundays were kept and you had your morning service at eleven o'clock where there was Bible reading and hymns were sung. All the work had to be done Saturday evening and you weren't allowed to go riding or skating on Sunday. The folks followed the commandments of Moses, "Thou shalt not—," so to speak. Perhaps they went to the extreme a little, yet I think a lot of their rules helped us along the way. Our parents were always reminding us to be honest and truthful and kind to others. So I think these were some of the things that helped us to be contented with one another and with what we had which wasn't very much, compared with what we have today.

Medical services

While I grew up in Mud Lake there were quite a few changes between 1907 and 1911. The Dickey Lumber Company moved out. I understood from my father they went bankrupt. The Grenfell Mission[3] served Groswater Bay and the fishermen along the coast from a hospital at Indian Harbour. When the Dickey Lumber Company moved out, Dr. Wakefield and Dr. Harry Paddon, who was a young man at that time, moved into Mud Lake. For the winter months they provided the Groswater Bay area with medical service and also travelled the coast north and south by dog team. Shortly after he came, Dr. Paddon married a nurse by the name of Minaly Gieldress. She came from the USA.

About 1914 they began to build a hospital in North West River. Later on they closed down Indian Harbour and Dr. Paddon started his work in North West River and there he raised a family of four sons: Tony, Harry, Richard and John. He was the only doctor.

I never really knew Sir Wilfred Grenfell. His work in Groswater Bay was about over, because Dr. Paddon took over for him. He served the coast some time after that, but I never knew him well. I met him a few times and that was all. He was a very pleasant person and devoted to the Labrador people. He was liked by all, according to our older folks.

Move to Sebaskachu

About that time, when the Grenfell Mission was stationed at Mud Lake for the winter months, my father moved our family to a place called Sebaskachu, about eighteen miles north of North West River. When we moved to this place there was one old man with his four sons living there. Two of the sons lived with their father. The two older ones were building homes because they were planning to get married. So there were three homes in this settlement. When my father built his home it made four.

Housing

The houses were built out of logs. The boards for the roof and floor were also ripped out of logs from a scaffold built about eight feet above the ground. The saw they used was called a bit saw. It was used by two men. One worked on top of the scaffold and one in under it. The saw itself was about ten feet long. Many times I sat on the ground and watched them do their work. The lumber that came from the saw was rough. It was laid on the floor that way and the women folk had to scrub it down with sand and cork and in about two months we had a good white floor that was free of splinters. We all had wooden floors in those days. There was no such thing as tiles or floor canvas. The walls were generally papered with newspapers or the wrapping paper you got on your parcels. There was no paper of any kind thrown away in those days.

The beds in our homes were made of wood and had bird-feather mattresses. They were very warm beds. The stoves were all wood stoves. Some of them were Waterloo cooking stoves, and some were box stoves. The box stoves were like two boxes one on top of the other. The bottom one was the fire box and the top was used for baking bread and cooking meals. The pots and kettles were all iron. The only way to keep them clean was to take them down to the water's edge and scour them with sand and a cloth.

Soap-making

Most of the soap was homemade from animal fat cooked with a lye liquid boiled from the ashes that we took from our wood stoves.

The lye was strong enough if it ate a piece of cloth when it was dipped into it for a minute. Then a big boiler was put on the stove and the fat was rendered out. We could not get tallow or pork fat or anything like that and had to use seal fat. The boiler was made of iron and had four legs.

Mother had me stand at the side of the stove for an hour each day pouring the lye into the fat a cup at a time until the fat was cooked. It took about seven days. When the soap was cooked she took about a half cup of coarse salt and about a pint of water to separate the soap from the lye. Then it was put away to cool for three days and then cut out in blocks.

After all this work we would get about three pounds of soap. By the time I got married we could buy Gillet's lye so I used to make my soap in fifteen minutes. I had it a lot easier. The lye soap was used for all the hard work—scrubbing floors and washing heavy clothes. There was no Dutch Cleanser. Our wood floors had to be scrubbed with sand and cork once a week. The Labrador girl learned to do all this kind of work when she was about twelve years old. People always had to keep working at something to make ends meet.

Food

The daily diet was made up of fresh meat and fish, peas and beans. Morning meals generally were rolled oats or fish. We did not have milk very often. Milk was only used for someone sick or at Christmas or Easter. Molasses was used for tea and on porridge. I tell you we were glad to see Christmas or Easter.

When Easter morning came there was coffee and milk on the table. When my father went back into the country in January he would send back about two pounds of candy by way of one of the dog teams carrying food and supplies in to the trappers. For two or three months we would get a piece of candy before going to bed at night.

Spring tonic

Under father's health rules we were treated with a spring tonic made from sulphur and molasses. This was to clean up any stomach worms. We took one teaspoon in the morning for a week and then stayed off it for a week and then took it for another week. This was during the month of May.

Father boiled spruce and juniper and we had to drink that with our dinner meal. It was a good drink. It was made of spruce, molasses, yeast, raisins and rice and tasted something like Coke. We had to drink that for a month to clean our blood. That was done every spring all the time we were growing up.

Then we had medicine from the trees that we used for cuts or burns or boils on our bodies. For boils we cut a juniper stick two inches in diameter and boiled it for three hours in pieces you could get in a pot. Then we took a piece and peeled off the outside bark. Under this there was another layer of a gummy mixture. We beat that to a pulp and made a poultice and used the liquid to bathe the infected place.

The only thing we had to eat in winter apart from our daily diet were berries. We would eat them every day. We used to pick them by the barrel. Dr. Paddon called them our "blood cleaner."

Grenfell Mission Spring Fair

Dr. Paddon was always busy. On his sick rounds he would also be preparing his songs for his yearly fair and concert. He was a good singer and a good actor. He always had one big sale about the twentieth of April. Everybody would gather in from around the Groswater Bay and join in the Grenfell Mission Spring Fair. The money was raised to help keep the Mission at work. The ladies would make handwork and the men would make pieces of furniture which would be put up for auction. Sometimes they would raise $700. Once they made $5,000. This was something the people looked forward to every year.

Santa Claus

Dr. Paddon always took time to think of the children at Christmas. I remember the first time I saw Santa. I was thirteen years old at the time. Dr. Paddon sent gifts to our home, eighteen miles from North West River, and had the old gentlemen put up a Christmas tree. He sent word around to my mother a week ahead and then brought Santa on his dog team all dressed up in his red suit. This was the first time our family saw a real Santa. This was one of the things Dr. Paddon did apart from his medical work.

When he came to visit he would often tell us a little about city life. Although we listened we didn't pay much attention because we knew nothing about it. He always ended up saying, "I am glad to be in Labrador and to be among the people. I love it here and all the beauty of its land, the mountains and all its trees and rivers." He would chat away in this manner and we enjoyed him very much. He was always a welcome guest in our home and I guess in all our homes because he was our only doctor at that time to travel the coast and look after our ills.

When he would leave us he always shook our hands and said to us, "Now children, eat all the meat and fish and red berries you can if you want to build strong bodies." This would be when he was leaving for his trip on the coast south. Then when he came back a month or six weeks later he would tell mother and father about the poor people and their problems and I sat and listened. He would say that the homes were so cold and they hadn't enough bedding and the food situation was very poor. There was little nourishment for the children and they were poorly dressed and I could see by the look on his face that he was very concerned about these problems. My mother and father were concerned too because their uncles, aunts and cousins were tied in with the situation, and they were saddened because Dr. Paddon couldn't take enough supplies for himself and the people. He had to travel as light as he could. The weather was cold and fierce to travel in, thirty and forty below zero most of the time, but I learned more and more that he was really concerned about the people and I always believed he loved them very much. His wife also was a wonderful helper to him and she was a good nurse, too.

I feel that Labrador really became a part of them. Dr. Paddon died in the United States, but his body was cremated and brought back to North West River and buried on the side of a little hill overlooking the waters of Groswater Bay. I admired him very much. He was a good straightforward man and we could always expect a good handshake from him.

Inflation

At the beginning of the First World War the cost of living went up awfully high. I remember my father coming home with his winter supplies and he told mother the flour was twenty-six dollars a barrel. That was 198 pounds. I can remember him telling mother we were only to have one slice of bread between meals and that we should eat as much meat and fish as we possibly could every day. That meant the children who were big enough had to fish and hunt rabbits. When the weather was fine the mothers of the families were always preparing boots and clothing and cooking the meals. So all the children who were old enough to work took part in the daily activities. We were up early in the mornings and to bed early at night.

Entertainment

Life was pretty rugged for a girl in Labrador. In my day there was not much around except lots of hard work. We didn't get much time for play. If we went out of the house we had to take the baby and look after it when we were playing so we were never free from some kind of work.

In the springtime we hunted birds' nests and we would go and see them every day until the little birds left their nests and flew away. There were no other children to play with so we had to do things like that to entertain ourselves. We were taught not to hurt birds or animals.

The only real entertainment we had was listening to Uncle Peter Michelin[4] playing square dance music on his violin and singing folk songs. People would gather in one house and have an evening singing. When I was fourteen years old my cousin came to our home and we drove eighteen miles to North West River for a New Year's square dance. We danced lances, cotillions and the Birdy Dance; the popular tunes were *The Soldier Boy*, *The Girl I Left Behind Me*, *The Irish Washerwoman* and others I don't know the names of. But the oldtimers were pretty good at playing their violins. There were no other musical instruments except mouth organs and a flute that Uncle Peter Michelin had. We would go to a New Year's dance and that would have to do until the next year came around.

Mail service

The mail service was not very regular. The best service was in summer. The mail steamer used to travel from St. John's to Rigolet. When we lived in the outports we did not get the mail very often. In winter the steamer came as far as Battle Harbour and mail was transferred all the way up the coast by dog teams as far north as Nain and up Groswater Bay as far as North West River.

Catching fish and birds

From 1914 to 1916 I was busy helping my father and mother. We had a hard struggle to survive. I was always preparing fish or meat to eat every day. There were no laws on killing wild birds or catching fish, so we would kill enough to eat every day and also preserve some in salt for the summer months. My father was a good hunter. He used to kill about 180 birds in the month of May and catch in nets about three or four hundred fish. These all had to be cleaned and put into barrels and used in the months of June, July and August. We never bothered to kill birds in these three months.

In August we would move down in the narrows of Rigolet to catch our winter's fish which were trout and codfish. They had to be cleaned and dried for the winter. We spent about one month down there in a cotton camp living in tents.

Summer hazards

The mosquitoes and black flies were numerous. We had to keep smoke in an old pot all day and keep the babies under a canopy made of cotton screen and hung over the bed. There were no insecticides to kill the flies. You had to put up with them for the months of July and August. After that we began to get frost at night and they died away.

At the end of August we would travel back up the bay and start to prepare ourselves again for winter. Our fathers brought home firewood for the winter and put it up in big piles for the three months they spent in trapping. The children of the home brought wood in every day for the night.

Our fathers left us then for three months and we didn't hear from them until they returned. Our mothers had to keep up courage and have faith in God to bring the men safely back to us again. We spent long winter nights thinking of our dads, hoping they would bring us home a good catch of furs. This was the only time we looked forward to getting a few candies or a Christmas gift. We only had them home for one month in mid-winter and then they returned again to their trapping grounds for three more months. This was the yearly routine for a trapper.

The girls in Labrador were expected to learn to mend and make their own clothes and boots just as soon as possible. There were no idle people out of work.

In 1917 I went to work for the Grenfell Mission in Indian Harbour and was paid four dollars a month and ten dollars worth of used clothing in the summer. This was what the mission gave their girls at that time. I served as an aide on the women's ward.

We were out of bed at five in the morning and on our feet until seven in the evening. We got one afternoon off week and we were let off to go to church on Sunday. This was where I met my first boy friend. We were allowed to take our boy friends into the kitchen in the evenings an entertain them with a record player. They had to leave a nine o'clock. We went to our rooms then and got ready for bed. I was only fifteen then and that was the first time I met Jim Goudie. Jim was cod fishing out there. We became good friends and went out together when I had my afternoon off. We enjoyed the summer very much. The time came to close down the hospital at the end of summer so Dr. Paddon moved some of the staff servant girls back to North West River for the winter to the hospital there. The Indian Harbour hospital was kept open until all the fishermen had gone back to Newfoundland for the winter so a part of the Grenfell staff stayed out there that year well on to the end of October and I was among the crowd. Jim had already gone back to North West River and into his trapping grounds. I didn't see him for some months after and we had only a very short visit in the spring of 1918.

Mrs. Paddon's children were small then. She had a nursemaid for them. The doctor and his wife had a little bungalow on the hill back of the hospital. The girls on staff that summer were the nursemaid Rachel Flowers and her helper Annie Baikie; the cook Kitty Montague; the parlour maid Beatris Flowers; and Jarmel McLean and I were the aides. The men's staff included Uncle Fred Blake, the two kitchen boys Austin Montague and John Montague; the crew on the *Yale*[5] were Judson Blake and Tom Elson. Either Dr. Paddon or Fred Blake went in the bay each trip the *Yale* made. Dr. Paddon went every trip if there were sick calls to make. He had two student doctors the summer I was there plus two nurses and his wife. There were fresh-air shacks on both wards that summer and they were always full of TB patients. One aide and one nurse were on duty all day. Dr. Paddon was a minister every Sunday as well as a doctor every day. Every man and woman in Labrador in those days who was able to work at all had to be a jack-of-all-trades. There was no other way out.

In 1918 my boy friend Jim Goudie joined the army and went to St. John's to train, but later that year the war ended. He did not get overseas. The war ended November 11 and my boy friend and his friend were brought to Battle Harbour by the mail steamer. They travelled the rest of the way up the coast by foot or dog team, when they could hire one. It was not until February that they got back to their own home village of North West River. There were others who returned later from overseas. This part of Labrador lost five young men in the First World

War: John Shiwak and William McKenzie from Rigolet, and John Blake, Daniel Groves and Charles Mesher from North West River and Mud Lake.

The war was over in November but we did not get the news until February when the two young men reach home.

3. Marriage To Trapper Jim Goudie

My boy friend and I used to meet each other about three times a year. We got engaged in February 1920 when he was going into the country. When he came out the first of April we set the date for our marriage. We were married on the twenty-first of April.

I learned when he came out of the country that he had almost lost his life. There were bad rapids in the river with open water and very thin ice to walk on. Donald Blake was with him. As they were trying to get their sleds around the rapids Jim's sled slipped off into the rapids and pulled him in too. He was driven down the rapids about a half mile in thirty below zero weather. The other man got him out after a while, but they were about a half mile from their cabin and Jim had to walk in his frozen clothes. He almost perished by the time he got there.

He stayed that night in the cabin for a rest. On the second of April he started for North West River. He had to travel forty miles on snowshoes carrying his load. Then he had to walk twenty-five miles more up Groswater Bay to the Hamilton River to get my father's and mother's consent before we could get married. I was at the head of Grand Lake, so he hired a dog team and sent up for me.

I arrived in North West River on April 16. I only had four days to get ready for the wedding. I had to make some of my wedding clothes, but I bought my dress from Mrs. Paddon. It cost me five dollars. It was a white dress with a little blue stripe in it. It is forty-three years now since I was married and I still have my dress.

On April 20, 1920, I was eighteen years old, and on April 21 we got married. It was a double-wedding ceremony. Two couples stood up at the one time. The Grenfell Mission nurse made our wedding cakes. We had quite a lot of people. We served a supper for everyone and we danced until three o'clock in the morning. My husband's brother played the violin. He had had TB and his right arm was cut off about six inches below his elbow. They tied the bow onto the stump of his arm and he played for our wedding dance. He could play the violin well. We stayed at his home for two weeks.

After that we moved to our own house which we bought from my father. It was a log cabin with two bedrooms and a kitchen. We walked eighteen miles to get to our home in Sebaskachu where my great-grandfather Michella had settled down when he first came to Labrador.

When I got married I did not have much money of my own. I had saved enough to buy myself a washboard. You will remember that I had worked for two dollars a month from the local people and four dollars a month from the Grenfell Mission. I had worked from the age of fourteen to the age of eighteen and although it was hard work I enjoyed it. I learned to keep house and cook, to make clothes, boots and shoes.

II
LIFE AS A
TRAPPER'S WIFE

The men they are a rare breed,
Who founded this great land.
They fished and trapped the waterways,
From the coast to far inland.

—from a song by Byron Chaulk

1. Early Married Life

So now I was starting all on my own. I had to do my best. I looked forward to a family of my own. It was two years before I started a family. In those two years I enjoyed myself with Jim. We used to go hunting and fishing. I learned to shoot with the gun. We enjoyed ourselves out in the quiet country.

I used to be left alone when he was away in the country. It was the most dreadful thing being a trapper's wife, as we would not hear from them from the time they would go away until they would return again. There was no way to get mail. The trappers would stay in the trapping grounds for a period of three months. We used to stand on the shore and watch them leave in their loaded canoes only six inches above the water. They would have to travel a lot by night when it was calm. The trappers would fire three or four shots from their guns and the men on the shore would answer them by shooting in return. That would be the last we would see of them for three months.

During the first year I was married I had lots of time on my hands. I would go hunting and fishing and in the long evenings I would read a book if I had one. Sometimes I would go out and visit our few neighbours. They would tell stories of the happenings in their lives and on Sundays everyone would stay in the house and rest. We would be glad to get a rest.

Mail service

Mail from Canada and Newfoundland was brought to Battle Harbour by the Newfoundland steamer and it would then have to travel up the coast by dog team. There were about four teams to cover the coast from Battle Harbour to Nain. Jim Saunders[6] was one of the men who helped take the mail from Makkovik to Nain. That's between eighty and ninety miles. It would take him about four days in fine weather and the pay was twenty dollars a trip. So you can see what it was like back in the early 1900s. I suppose it was more complicated before that.

Midwife at eighteen

During the first year I was married there was a woman expecting a baby and the nearest midwife was about twenty miles away. The woman's family were going to get the midwife two weeks before the baby was due, but a cold snap of weather came and the waters partly froze up. They could not get the midwife. It was in November when the baby came and I had to act as midwife. I got along all right with the help of an old man who was there. I was so afraid I would lose the mother or the baby. I was sick in bed for three days after, but the mother lived and her son lived also.

Winter fish supply

These were the kind of things we had to go through to live and get along in Labrador. As time moved on and I recovered from the shock, the ice completely froze over. I went to catch trout for my winter. I walked four miles and carried enough food for a week. I caught about 500 trout. I built a scaffold and put my trout up where the little animals could not get at them and covered them over with boughs of the trees so the birds could not steal them. I went back home for a while until the ice was nice and strong. Then I took my sled and went back and hauled them home. I had plenty of trout for my winter. That's what I did to pass the time while Jim was away at his hunting ground. Shortly after I had that finished he arrived home. All was well and he had done fairly well with fur. That was in January.

Return from trapping

The custom for trappers' wives is to have something cooked for their husbands when they come home. We used to have pie and cake and then they would rest up for a week. We went to North West River to sell Jim's furs after he had a rest. I put on my snowshoes and went with him. We had two or three days there and then returned home. Jim rested up for a month and then went back into the country again.

Winter life

In the cold of winter we had to stay in the house a lot. My hobby was knitting and sewing and preparing boots for spring. I used to go out for long walks in fine weather. We always had to bring in all our wood and water. At Sebaska-chu where we lived first, we were near the salt water and I had to bring in blocks of snow and melt it for water. Out of about ten pounds of snow you would get about a quart of water. We would have to do our laundry and cleaning and everything with snow water. To make forty-five gallons you would have to use about 1,800 pounds of snow, and that would last two days. We would keep adding blocks of snow to the barrel to keep up the stock of water.

That was the daily routine as we lived it. We would only see a minister or doctor about once in the winter. Outside of that we would have to look after our own sores or cuts the best way we could throughout the year. You would be surprised what you can do when you have to do without the doctor. We sterilized our rags for cuts and infections by browning them on the stove.

Spring bird-hunting

As the winter moved on and spring came the bird-hunting season opened. We used to go hunting by canoe. The canoes were painted white to hide them from the birds. People wore white coats and caps and made white cotton coverings for the canoe paddles. They would hide behind a wood frame lined with white cotton built up about two feet above the canoe. That was how they would paddle up to the birds. They would paddle up to about fifty yards and kill them on the first shot. This would last about three weeks after the first of June. Then there was no more hunting because the birds would lay their eggs and people would not hunt birds anymore until September. That was the custom of the country. Everybody kept it.

Summer salmon fishing

Summer 1920 came and we were planning a boat trip ninety miles down the Hamilton[7] to Rigolet. There were many people down there. It was salmon-fishing time and all the people went there for the summer. We went down just to spend the summer among them as we really had nothing to do. We started off in a fourteen-foot boat with sails on her but we would row when it was calm. There were lots of places to explore on the way. It was a good trip—nice land and little rivers where we did some fishing. The first night we camped just when it was getting dark. The mosquitoes were plentiful. Everywhere you went in summertime you had to carry a canopy to put over your bed to keep the flies out. We travelled many miles a day. It took about seven days to get to Rigolet. We spent the month of July down there.

While we were at Rigolet there was an eclipse of the sun lasting about six hours. I had to light my lamp, it was so dark in the house. We have a lot of Indian Tea[8] in our country and it bears little white flowers. During the eclipse they were a pale blue. I had gone out to fetch some water from a well when I discovered the flowers were blue. It was on a Saturday. I was making a pair of boots for Jim. I had to make them in the lamplight.

The land around us was hilly and barren. We climbed the hills and picked berries. We always found something to do every day. While we were there we caught our fish for the winter and dried them. By the time we got that finished it was about the middle of August. We all went to Rigolet for the round-up of the year. It was the custom of the fishermen when the fishing season was over to have a big dance. We spent two or three nights dancing and then everyone broke up for another year.

We started up the bay. On our way up we stopped at Es-kimo Island. My mother had told me that all the Eskimos had died some years before from a disease they got from a ship that was wrecked on the rocks in the mouth of the Hamilton Inlet. They found the ship after everyone else had gone to their trapping places so they had no help from anyone. They all died and nobody knew anything about it until the next spring. They found all the graves and food and materials. We wanted to know if there were any signs of the disaster left. We stayed overnight and explored the island. We found about 100 graves. Some of the remains were covered over with ground, but some were still on top of the ground. There were leg bones and backbones lying on top of the ground under rocks, still not decayed. We dug some beads out of the ground and pieces of clothing.

Return from Rigolet

We started back to our winter place. We got about five miles, but had to camp because it began to blow. We got up in the morning and started again. We went about seven miles and stopped to pick some berries. That was the fifteenth of August. We had about forty-five miles of a big open bay yet to go. We had to travel by night most of the time because it was blowing too hard in the day.

We moved on at about the rate of five miles a night. We used to rest by day and have our fun and explore the new land. We saw many young ducks and geese squawking. We had plenty of amusement every day, nice fresh berries and pretty, dribbling brooks. We were not lonely, we were happy. Of course, I had gotten away from a lot of the work. I had lots of time for the things around us.

As we were rowing along one night a goose honked. The noise was right alongside us so Jim stopped the boat and picked up his gun. We waited until we could see signs of the birds swimming on the water by the light of the sky. Jim shot where he saw something on the water and the geese flew away. We rowed ahead and looked where he had fired the shot. He had killed one, so we had fresh goose meat for dinner next day. It was good.

After we got about forty miles up the widest part of the bay we travelled faster. It's about twenty miles across, so it can get pretty rough when it blows hard. We finally reached home after travelling fifteen days. I was tired and weary from our trip.

Winter 1921

It was then the first of September, and we had just a month to get everything ready for winter. Jim was busy getting his wood home and sawing it up for the winter and I went about making boots and clothes for him. We had to make two shifts of clothing. We always prepared extra things in case of accidents like fires or losing the canoe in the river. The trapper's wife took a month to get her husband ready and this was my first year. We didn't have much time for fun. We worked early and late. The day came for Jim to leave. That was a very sad day for a trapper's wife.

You may think there was nothing left to do when our men were gone. But each day brought its work. We didn't have time to be too lonely. We were always busy. The night-time was lonely. Not a person to speak to. We would go to bed early. A trapper's life was not a lonely one because each day brought sights and new life. His wife would spend a more lonely time. She was always at home, but there was something about that life that is hard to put into words. It was a life not full of people or what people could offer you. You would rise in the morning. There were no people around you, but every day you had something to make you happy. We were satisfied. We did not get fed up with our lives. We were people who never had a lot of money. We would just live from day to day. We never worried about it. We always said if God wants us to live he will provide for us, as long as we do our part. We were content with that thought. I never stopped to think about my mother's life as a young trapper's wife when I was young, but when I was married I learned all about it. The first year I was married was a very lonely one. I was only eighteen years old.

First baby

My second year looked brighter. There was a baby on the way. When Jim left for his trapping ground he left me in care of my mother. Jim came back from the country in April and I moved to North West River. My baby was due in May and there was a doctor there. Jim thought I should be near the doctor. When the time came I didn't go into the hospital. There was a midwife there. On 14 May, 1922, I had my first son. He weighed eight-and-a-half pounds and was just like his daddy. He had a dark complexion and I was proud of him. When he was seventeen days old I had to take him to the doctor because he had sore eyes. The doctor asked me his name. I didn't have a name then, so the doctor looked at the baby, and as he was hairy about his shoulders and neck the doctor said he would call him Esau. So his name in the hospital book at North West River is Esau, but later I named him Horace.

2. Life On Labrador's North Coast

That spring shortly after Horace was born we decided to move farther north. When my baby was three months old we left North West River and started our trip to Hopedale. A few days before we left I took sick, but I managed to look after the baby. We had to travel in an open motorboat about ninety miles down the Hamilton Inlet. When we got to Rigolet I was getting worse. We got a room in one of the Hudson's Bay houses and had to wait for the mailboat to come from St. John's, Newfoundland. We had to wait ten days, and I was getting worse every day. At last I was in bed. The boat arrived and I went aboard. There was a nurse aboard who told me I had yellow jaundice. She said I had better go to the hospital at Indian Harbour. There I was with a small baby and sick myself. I talked it over with Jim and we didn't have the means and ways to pay someone to look after the baby. I had no choice but to go on with my husband. The nurse gave me a list of what to eat to help myself. On the boat I could get fresh fruit and vegetables and I began to recover.

Arrival in Hopedale

When we got to Hopedale and had to leave the boat I didn't know what to expect for my baby. We were among strangers there. Most of them were Eskimos. There

were a few settlers and the Moravian missionaries. Jim's
brother Charlie was there waiting for us. The day after
we landed at Hopedale Jim had to go in Ujutok Bay and
start building. It was about the twentieth of August and
we had to build a house for the winter. The week he was
gone I got very sick. I had to take to my bed. The young
ladies in the home we stayed in took my baby and cared
for him. I got so sick the mother of the family went to the
Moravian missionaries and they sent me three big white
pills and three doses of Epsom salts. After I took that I
got better. I was miles from my home, among strangers,
but they were very kind to me.

Home in Ujutok Bay

The next week I moved up the bay where they had the
logs ready to start building the house. I was the only
woman in those forty miles from Hopedale. I stayed in a
cotton camp about two months with my small baby and
waited for the house to be built. I never saw anyone until
Charlie, Jim's brother, went to Makkovik in the fall after
the house was finished and got a housekeeper for himself.
I was glad I had company.

When the men went to their trapping lines we were
all alone for two months. We had to carry in all our water and wood. The black bears were plentiful and there
were some wolves around too. We would hear the wolves
howling and saw some bears pass by. We kept our guns
loaded all the time.

Eskimo neighbours

I was only twenty years old then. Ellen, Charlie's cook,
was a good shot with a rifle and she taught me how to shoot

because she would go away hunting all day sometimes and I would be left alone with my small baby. Jim and Charlie were away on their trapping lines. There were no settlers in that bay. The closest people were at Hopedale. Sometime in late fall two Eskimo families moved into the bay. It was about Christmas time when we found out they were about three miles from us, so when Jim and Charlie returned from their trapping, Ellen and I put on our snowshoes and went to visit them. One family had gone to Hopedale for Christmas but the other family was there. They could not speak English. Ellen could understand them a little. They were awfully glad to see us and when we left they wanted to give us something. They took a partridge out of the pot they had cooking on the stove and gave it to us. They were the first people I had seen since August.

As the weather got colder we discovered our house was very cold. I was worried because of my baby. When January came the men had to go into the country.

January 1923

It was the beginning of 1923. By this time Charlie had made up his mind to marry his cook and they wanted to spend their honeymoon in the country. Jim had to look for a place for me to stay with the baby so he took the dog team and went to the next bay where William Mitchell lived. His mother was an Englishwoman. I stayed with these people for two months.

I had it nice there and they got along very well with me. They had servants. It was very comfortable. The girls of the family were grown up and they just about took over the baby and looked after it. I had time to go fishing and hunting; I had time to read books. I enjoyed myself very much.

The time came around for Jim to come home and I had to move back again. It was lonely again because Ellen, Charlie's wife, was a great outdoors-woman, and she would be away with her husband every day. I would be home alone, only me and my baby. I would see the wolves passing by during the day and I was afraid of them. I would have to do my outdoor work when my baby was asleep.

Spring 1923

By this time my baby was growing bigger and I enjoyed him more. Soon he was beginning to walk. April came and the trapping season was over. Jim was home again. Charles and Ellen were also home. It was not so lonely then. I was beginning to get out more as I had someone to stay with the baby when I wanted to see the land around where we lived. Across the bay I found an open water place about a mile long. I looked around for trout because there was a nice brook there. I found some lovely big ones; some of them would weigh two to three pounds. I caught plenty to eat.

Later on in the spring, around the first of May, about two thousand sea gulls moved into this open water place. Early in the morning the gulls would start to call and they would keep everyone awake, including the baby. At about four o'clock Jim would go out for his morning hunt. Horace, the baby, would want to get up and have a look at the gulls. There were so many of them hovering in the skies and calling and making a noise that I had to get up about six o'clock and take the baby downstairs and put him by the window where he could see them and I would do all my morning's work. Then I would take him down from the window and bathe him and he would have his morning sleep.

Charles was not satisfied with his furs. He did not get many that winter. When the ice broke up for the summer and the mailboat started its run north to Hebron, he packed up everything and took his wife up to Hebron.

We were left alone. We had to do something. When the mailboat started to travel north we wrote to Archie Goudie, another brother of Jim's, at Davis Inlet. We got an answer back saying there was lots of room for trapping where he was. We made up our minds to move to Davis Inlet.

Trip to Hopedale

In June we decided to make a trip to Hopedale by canoe. We had a fourteen-foot Peterborough canoe. We took our camp and started. We went about twenty miles the first day and camped. We saw lots of ducks—mostly eider ducks from the ocean. They are very pretty. The drake is white with some green on its head and neck and the hen is brown like a black duck. We saw lots of seals, too. They were in companies[9] of about fifty to a hundred in one lot. I was afraid of them because we were only in a small canoe. They would come as close as twenty feet from the canoe. It was early in the morning when we saw the seals. Jim said it was their feeding time. They came to the top of the water so thick that they were like sardines in a tin. Jim told me that in the early morning the caplin come to the top of the water. These are tiny fish seals feed on.

We had to cross a bay fifteen miles wide. There were seals everywhere. I did not feel very brave. Jim said there was no danger that they would attack us. I mustered up my courage and tried to be brave. Horace, my baby, was asleep during all of this. We were both paddling the canoe.

Jim said by the look of the sunrise in the morning and the clouds in the sky it would be a calm day. He was right. He travelled so much and went so much by the signs in the sky and the sunrises that he could tell what kind of a day we would have and he hardly ever made a mistake. It kept calm and we didn't lose any time. Jim was a good paddler and we travelled at the rate of about five miles an hour. When I paddled with him we travelled at the rate of about seven miles an hour.

At about eleven o'clock in the morning my baby would wake up and I had to give up paddling and nurse him. He wriggled about and tried to climb over the side of the canoe while I was nursing him.

I had a chance to see everything. The birds and seals were so plentiful that I forgot all about my fear and enjoyed myself very much. At noon we reached an island about halfway across. It was still calm. Jim said we would go on shore and have lunch and a rest. We stayed about an hour. He said the tide was high and if it was going to blow the wind would blow on the high tide at one o'clock. It was still calm at half past one. We started again. My baby was asleep and I could paddle now. We had to go about eight more miles to reach the north side of the bay. We paddled with all our strength and at about five o'clock in the evening we reached the shore. I was pretty sure we would be safe now because we could follow the shore the rest of the way to Hopedale. We set up our camp again. It was the second day since we had left home. Horace was getting tired of the trip. It was a long trip for a baby. We had long evenings of daylight in June with sunlight lasting until nearly eleven o'clock.

I went about cooking supper. We had some ducks we had killed on the trip. Jim was looking for water and wood because the land was just about barren. There were not many trees in sight and we were surrounded by salt water. Jim got back with water and wood and soon I had supper cooked. This was the first cooked meal in two days. We had to travel while it was calm and therefore never took the time to cook a meal. Anyway when supper was ready we really enjoyed it. It was about seven o'clock when we finished supper and we had about four hours of daylight left.

Jim went about preparing the camp for the night. He chopped the wood and fetched the water. I was busy with my baby; I had to heat water for his bath and do his laundry. I had two days' laundry to do for him by this time. I got all that done and it was about ten o'clock. We still had an hour of daylight. Jim had everything ready for the night. We went inside the tent and spread our bedding and went to rest for the night. We were both very tired. The baby was very happy then. He had had his bath and his supper and he was dressed in all clean clothes. He was ready for bed again and crawled in beside us and fell asleep.

We talked for a while. Jim asked me if I was afraid that day crossing the bay. I said I was very much afraid. He told me he knew by the sunrise that morning it was going to be a calm day. He went on and explained some things about his travels to me which I didn't understand. He told me that the trappers learned to travel by the signs in the sky. They knew weather was going to blow or be calm by the colour of the sunrise and clouds in the sky. I tried to learn something about travelling for myself. From the experience that I went through that day I saw that there was a lot to learn.

Jim and the baby were asleep now and I could not get to sleep. I lay awhile in the tent and then I went outside.

It was just beginning to get light. It was about one o'clock now. I went for a long walk. The sky was so beautiful and clear and the water was so calm that I was just lost in the beauty of everything around me. The land was rugged and bare, but it was beautiful. The little birds were waking up for the morning. The squirrels and rabbits were pouncing about the side of the hill. I looked up and the sun was rising. I thought I had better get back to the camp. When I got back it was two o'clock. I was away an hour but it had only seemed about ten minutes. Jim and the baby were still asleep. I lay down and fell asleep myself.

I never knew anything until Jim woke me at six o'clock. He had breakfast ready. We had our breakfast and started to break camp; the weather was still fine so we took our time. I had to get my baby ready. I dressed him for the day and gathered up all his laundry which I had spread about on the rocks the night before. It was all nice and dry. My baby was happy as a bee. He was thirteen months old then. We left about eight o'clock the third day hoping to reach Hopedale that evening. We had about twelve miles to go. I didn't paddle much because Jim said we had lots of time to reach Hopedale. I took a rest and just looked after my baby. It was a nice morning again as we started out. The same thing happened around us that day as the days before. There were lots of seals and ducks so we had plenty of company. There were no people, but many wild animals and birds. We didn't see a person for three days. There were no liveyers[10] around that part of the bay.

Shortly after we left the shore we saw a large, black bear come out of the woods and have his breakfast. He was feeding on caplin. These small fish, about five inches long, come right onto the beach to spawn. You will find these little fish in openings in the cliffs or in small coves rolling in on the beach about four feet deep in some places. You could see them from the boat 500 yards away. I didn't know what it was until Jim told me and the black bear was out in the water right up to his stomach feeding on them.

Arrival at Hopedale

As the day passed by we were nearing the Moravian Station at Hopedale. At about three o'clock in the afternoon we could see it in the distance. My mind was relieved. I had been sitting in that canoe for three days with my thirteen-month-old baby, not able to move five inches to the right or to the left or I would have turned the canoe over and we would all have been drowned. You can imagine the strain my body was under. I was so relieved when I saw the station that I fell asleep and we were at Hopedale when I awoke at four o'clock.

The people were on the wharf to greet us with smiling faces, and we were also very glad to see them. We were taken in to Mr. William Mitchell. These were the first people we had seen for months. It was quite a treat to see people again. There were only two English-speaking families there beside the Moravian missionaries. Most of the population were Eskimos. We stayed a few days in Hopedale. It was about the last of June in 1923.

There was a letter awaiting us from Archie, wanting us to buy a motorboat. Jim looked around among the boats and found one about thirty feet long with an engine. It was great for me because I did not have to go back in the canoe.

The summer seasons are not very long up north, so we started back to our house on the second of July. We made our trip in one day in the motorboat. We picked up our few things and started back for Davis Inlet. We had to pass through Hopedale again to get to Davis Inlet. We lost no time and went straight on. It took us three days along the coast. Jim was a stranger to the coast, so the people in Hopedale told him what route to follow. Again we were going into a strange place. We made our trip all right and never struck a reef of rocks.

House building

We arrived at Davis Inlet on July 6. Archie Goudie was out in the bay salmon-fishing. We had to wait for him. It was two weeks before we got to our winter place in Merrifield Bay. We had to build two houses before winter came. They cut all the logs and sawed the lumber for the roofs and floors by hand. We moved into the bay and put up our camp. I had to live in a camp the rest of the summer waiting for our house to be built.

The work was slow. The mosquitoes were so plentiful that we had to keep smoke in front of the door of our camp every day and use a mosquito net over our heads. This was the second summer I had camped out waiting for a house to be built. My baby was going into his second year. This condition of life was getting pretty boring, but I had to stick with it. Jim built a cookhouse where we could bake our bread and prepare meals. We did all the laundry by hand. There was no water close by; we had to carry it about 100 yards. Whenever my baby left my arms to sleep, he had to be put under a net. The flies would have killed him if he was left uncovered.

You would not see grown dogs in summer. They would live under the rocks or in holes in the ground to keep alive. They would feed themselves in summer. There would be lots of fish driven into the shallow water. The dogs would be seen in the daytime feeding along shore, but you never saw them in the evening. They would go back to their caves again. Then after the flies were gone they would come back home and up over their eyes and around the ears and around their tails they would be picked to the bare flesh. This might sound hard to believe, but it's true. We lived up there seven summers. When I saw the dogs like that I wondered how I was going to keep my children alive.

The worst month for mosquitoes is July. We didn't see much of the flies that summer because when we moved into the bay it was about the last week in July. By then most of the flies were gone.

We didn't have a dog team of our own. We just had one female pup and had to raise a team of our own. By the second year we had three male pups with the mother. She was a real Eskimo dog, a big dog. The second year we had a team of six. Jim looked after them well. Eskimo dogs need to be well-fed and well-disciplined. You want them to know that their master is boss. We learned from people that you could not keep small pups in July. The flies would kill them. We lived near Robert Ford and his family. Their dog had a brood of pups and he didn't know it. One day he found two of the pups dead. He had to take the rest of them and put them under smoke from a smoke pot. He used to keep them near the door where he could watch them day and night until the flies left. The flies are not as bad as the mosquitoes.

As summer went by we were all busy getting ready to build our homes. Every spare moment I had I peeled the rind (bark) off the logs and helped to lay the floor. Archie's wife Lily could not do much, as she was a cripple. She used to mind the baby while I helped the men do the work. By September we had the floor laid and the walls of one house up. We built the biggest one first. It was twenty feet wide and twenty-four feet long.

Jim gets sick

Everything was going well, but Jim had a lot of fly bites on the back of his neck. One turned bad and his neck began to rise in a big lump. It was getting worse every day. He worked on about a week, but at last he had to give up. I could see it was going to be a boil. Two days after he stopped work he was wracked with pain. I was worried and there was no help within sixty-five or seventy miles (Nain).

The only thing left to do was to try juniper. My mother had told me how to prepare it. You cut a tree about two inches in diameter and saw it up so it is just big enough to get into a boiler. You boil it about four hours. Then you take it from the liquid and peel the rind off the outside. Inside there is a gummy pulp. You peel that off and make a poultice.

By this time I could see it was not an ordinary boil. It was a large carbuncle. I went to work with the poultice. I kept hot poultices on his neck every hour in the daytime and twice at night. It took seven days to bring it out with the poultice. The last three days he never slept or ate. I was almost sick myself. He was running a high temperature. At twelve o'clock on the seventh night he said to me that he was going to lie down; he could not sit up any longer. I could see that he was growing weaker by the hour. I made up the bed and tried to make him comfortable. He wasn't down very long before he fell asleep. I watched him and by one o'clock I could see the pus running down his neck. I thanked God for the relief. I knew then it was broken. I could manage.

I changed the dressing then and he never woke up. The pus was coming out in seven little holes. I lay down and fell asleep. We slept until morning. When Jim awoke he was feeling better. I had to change the dressing again. Before I could get him his breakfast he was feeling fine. Then he ate some breakfast and afterwards fell asleep again. I felt that the worst was over. The second morning he wanted to go to work. I managed to keep him in for three days. On the fourth day he went back to work.

He worked every day. The core was still in the middle of the carbuncle. It was a large one and it was deep. I continued with the juniper poultices. Every morning when I would dress it I would take a hair from my head and run it over the skin surface. I would get out a little piece of the core with my hair and a sterilized darning needle. That was how I removed the core from the carbuncle. It took me ten days before I got it all out. It healed up nicely. He never got any infections after that.

It was then about the twenty-fifth of September. Everyone was working early and late to get on with the houses. Mine wasn't started yet, but Archie's house was almost finished. Everything was going well.

The baby gets sick

In the second week in October my baby took sick. He woke up one morning with a high temperature and a cough. On the third day he was very sick. The only place where we could get any help was at Nain, sixty-five miles away. The Moravian Station missionary was a doctor. Jim was new to the coast and didn't know the way. He had to go and look for a pilot. He got back with the pilot the fourth day at about dinner time.

We started for Nain in the afternoon. When I took Horace up in my arms he was so sick he didn't know us when we spoke to him. The pilot said he didn't know if he would live to get to Nain. He said he would take us if we wanted to go. We said we would go and we started.

I was almost out of myself with worry about my sick child. It was about three o'clock in the afternoon. It seemed so awfully long, that sixty-five miles with my little boy almost dying. Our boat was not very good and the engine was not dependable. There was a lot to think about in the next twenty-four hours. The baby was still unconscious when we left the shore. I prayed that God would spare my child. We had to stop over at the pilot's house that night. When we arrived his wife had supper ready for us. There was still no change in my sick baby. I watched him very closely all the evening. He was just lying there, just breathing and that was about all. At about twelve o'clock at night he opened his eyes and seemed a little better. I gave him a drink and he fell asleep again.

Four o'clock in the morning came and we got up and started on our way. It was blowing from the northwest but not too hard. As the day came on the wind seemed to rise. We kept going all day. We didn't go ashore to make lunch; we boiled the kettle on board. We travelled all day without a stop, finally arriving at Nain just at dark.

My baby was still alive and he seemed a little better. We went straight to the missionary. After he examined the baby he told us he had double pneumonia but was over the worst of it. He further said there was a chance of him getting well again if I would be very careful with him and give him his treatments as the doctor instructed. We stayed in Nain three days and the doctor looked after him for me. On the fourth day he was much better and we started home again.

Fall 1923

When we arrived home Archie had the roof on his house and we moved in with the baby. It was then October and our house still had to be built. The logs were cut and the lumber sawed for the roof and floor. Jim said we didn't have time to build a very big one. He built one twenty feet by eighteen feet. We had a small bedroom and a kitchen. Both families lived in one house until ours was built. I never cared to live in the same house with another woman, and she was not a very pleasant woman to live with. I made up my mind to live there until my home was built. Besides my sick baby I was expecting my second baby. I had a lot on my mind.

October went by and November too. I still was not in our new house. We were lucky enough to have good weather. There was not very much snow that fall and it wasn't too cold. The trapping season was open and the men had to tend their traps. One week Jim would go on the trapping lines and Archie would work on our house. The next week Archie would go and Jim would work. I would be working too. I helped to put the floor down. I could drive nails pretty well. I picked moss which we put between the logs as insulation. On the fourteenth of December Jim came in late at night from working on the house. He told me that we would be able to move in the next evening.

Move into new house

We moved in and kept fires burning all night to keep it warm. We had gone north in 1922, and it was not until

December 15, 1923 that I had a house to call my own. It was not much of a house to look at, but it was a mansion to me. It was my own.

By now my baby was back to normal. Everything was fine. Jim was not home very much after he finished the house. He was away hunting meat and fish to keep us eating. I was busy catching up on my work, washing dishes, making boots and clothes and preparing meat and fish to eat. To be a trapper's wife and keep up with all the chores you have to work from six in the morning to nine at night. I never had time to read a book. I would get a little free time on Sunday afternoon. But what bothered me most was that I could only get letters about twice a winter from my family back home. In the daytime I would amuse myself by looking out at the bay and watching the wolves walking back and forth. Sometimes you would see a fox. Some nights when it was bright, clear weather there were lots of northern lights, and we would sit and watch them. There was one hill the lights would especially play around. They would come down so low that we could see the hill through the lights. So we named the hill Northern Light Hill. It went by that name after that.

Second baby born

On February 15 the second baby arrived. It was a girl, weighing seven pounds. We named her Marie. Our boy Horace was able now to run all over the place. When the new baby arrived he was not too pleased. One time he was eating a crust of bread and we heard the baby making a noise. Jim went and looked and Horace had put a piece of his bread in her mouth. We had to watch him closely after that.

I had to stay in bed for ten days after my baby was born. That was Dr. Paddon's instruction to the midwives—keep the mother in bed for ten days. Jim took over for me. He did the cooking, baked the bread, did the laundry and scrubbed the floor. He was very proud of his little girl. She seemed to be his favourite girl in the family. I wondered if his love for her would last and as the years rolled on, I learned that in our lives she really was his favourite. We went through so many hardships that year—we had no home to call our own and we almost lost our boy with pneumonia. I think she was special to us. We both loved her very much.

Bad water supply

As winter moved on we discovered that we had bad water. The water was very good when there was lots of rain, but we found out later in the spring that the water was coming out of the marsh back of us. A rust-coloured ochre powder lay all over the marsh in the spring. Jim and Archie took some home and dried it and mixed it with some linseed oil. They painted the motorboat with it and it stayed on a long time.

We learned that winter that we were going to have to move again. The men made sure the water was good the next time we moved. When summer came we pulled down our house and rebuilt it again when we moved. We settled on an island beside an old Englishman, Robert Ford, and his Eskimo wife Agusta. I had company, someone to talk to. His wife couldn't talk English, but she could talk a blend of English and Eskimo. I felt better knowing someone was around. They were very fond of my two children. We got along together very well and that's where we lived for the next four years.

It was a nice place, lots of birds and salmon in the summertime. There were lots of seals for our boots and lots of berries. The old lady who lived beside us was always out picking berries or cutting wood for her cooking stove. She had no family and she liked to be out-of-doors. She would give me some berries. Then in turn my husband would kill fresh meat for them. They were very pleased because the old gentleman was in his seventies and he could not see very well. They were good company and meant a lot to me.

Winter 1924

During the first winter we were there we had water problems again. The water was good, but it was not too plentiful. There was no mainstream of fresh water within four or five miles. There were just little dribbling brooks, running down the hillside. In winter that would freeze into ice. We would have to chop the ice off and haul it home on a *kamutik*[11] in a barrel and melt it into water. I had the two babies to do laundry for and that meant extra work for me. In the evenings I had to leave my children and go and bring ice for the next day. I did it while they were having a sleep. I was away from the house about half an hour. When they were awake I would get the old gentleman to babysit for me.

I was never really able to get away from home at all, winter or summer, without my children. I nursed all my babies. I never gave them the bottle. I was a lucky mother because I was hefty and able to nurse them for ten months. Then I would wean them from the breast and put them on meat gravies and fish.

I had an aunt who could not nurse her babies. She had to get a bottle for them. What she used for food was flour. She took the dry flour and packed it in a white cloth and boiled it for four hours. When she took it from the cloth it was like a piece of chalk that you use for the blackboard in school only it weighed about a pound. She would take a piece and grate it up and make a pap like a real thick gravy. She boiled it again and added sugar, a little butter and a little salt. She raised eight children like that until they were ten months old. Then she gave them meat gravies and fish. Some of them grew up to be old men and women. When put to the test we could always manage.

I was about nine years old when my mother showed me a piece of the pudding that my aunt used. It was white and she said it was still useable. She made some pap and tasted it. I would not like to have to eat it.

Many times my aunt was half-starving and poorly clothed. Her husband didn't have a very good trapping place and didn't know how to manage trapping well. It was not until their sons were old enough to go up the Hamilton River to make a trapping place that she had a better time. Then she did not live many years after that. When she was about forty years old she took TB. She only lived four more years and died when her youngest child was about four years old. The child died before he was twenty-one with TB of the throat.

Winter 1924–25

1925 arrived and I was expecting my third child. The winter was not very good. The furs were scarce. My husband was quite worried because there was nothing in sight for the summer. By spring we were hoping and praying something would turn up that would bring in a little money. Jim came out of the country from his traps and still didn't have many furs. I was in the fourth month with child. Jim went to Davis Inlet to the Hudson's Bay store and sold the few furs he did have. He brought home some food. It really was not enough for the spring. That meant Jim would have to spend the whole spring hunting and fishing.

Late in the spring he went out near the coastline and got a few seals. I cleaned them and sold the skins to the Hudson's Bay Company. The skins averaged about four dollars apiece. That provided a little more food. We managed until open water.

We made a few trips up Upitik River tending the black bear traps. We killed a seal one trip up the river. Horace was very excited about it and Marie, our little girl, was afraid of it. When we got to the bear trap, there was a bear in it. We took the children onto the bank of the river to look at the bear and Marie would have walked right over if we had let her. Horace ran back down to the canoe and would not look at the bear. All the way home, he sat back with his dad and would not touch it. Marie put her hands through the fur and played with it. It was about three o'clock when we got to the last trap, had our lunch and started back home. I did not paddle going back because we had the current of the river with us.

Everything was getting green and very beautiful. I was always a person who liked the scenery so I enjoyed my day very much, It took all day until about four o'clock to get to the last trap. The river was high and the current on it was very strong. We had lunch and started back. We had a great ride down the river with the tide. We reached the bay and we had to paddle. It was getting late. We were about six miles from home; we paddled on and at ten in the evening it was still day—the sun was shining. About eleven o'clock it was completely dark. We left again at 12:30 and it was getting a little light. We paddled on; we were about two miles from home. When we arrived home at 2:30, it was just like daytime. We reached home and the children were sleepy and tired and I put them to bed. I helped Jim take the bear and the seal out of the canoe and put everything away. We went to bed around four o'clock and got up again at nine. We had to skin the bear and seal and put them into water before the flies would spoil the fur. You could not put anything down for thirty minutes before the blue flies would blow in it and breed maggots. It would spoil in a short time. We had a busy day with all the usual daily chores beside that.

Summer 1925

In summer Jim got a cod-fishing place from Walter Bromfield. We managed, although there weren't many fish and we had no cod trap. Jim had to use hook and line. The prices were not very good, only seven dollars a quintle (112 pounds). We had to take out food on credit from the Hudson's Bay Company. That's how we lived that summer. We were all out on the coastline at a place called Tikkle. It's between Davis Inlet and Hopedale.

While we were there a trader came through Tikkle with food supplies. We went aboard and had a look around. We could not buy any food because we had no money. We had some fish and the trader would have bought them and given us a better price than the Company, but we had to keep our fish to pay off our credit bill. The food we took out for the summer had to be paid for.

A man by the name of Mr. Percy owned the sailing schooner with the food supplies from Newfoundland. He had everything on board to eat. That night when I went to bed I could see it before my eyes. My stomach just longed to taste that food.

It was late in June and we were having very warm weather. We had seventy-five and eighty degrees of heat some days. The flies were terrible. We had to keep smoke in a kettle by the door all summer long. When it was calm weather, I used ground sods and the rind and chips from the firewood and blackberry leaves. Blackberry leaves made the mildest smoke. It was not as hard on the eyes.

Baking bread

I forgot to tell how I did my baking. We only had a camp stove. I had to make flat cakes of flour and salt and baking powder. We were there for six weeks. One day I said to Jim, "I am tired of eating flat cakes." Jim called them flat jacks. I think that was the name the hunters used for them. Anyway, while we were talking about the cakes he said to me, "Mix a bread of yeast and I'll bake it for you." I said, "How are you going to bake without an oven?" He answered, "Never mind that, just get the bread ready." When I had it ready he said to put it in our big iron pot with a cover. Then he left for a while. I did not know where he was. When he came back for the bread I followed him and he had a fire built in a hole in the sand. He hooked all the hot fire brands out and put the iron pot in the hole and buried it with hot sand. I was afraid my bread was going to be spoiled. He said to leave it for an hour. I went back to the camp and waited an hour. He brought the pot back and I was afraid to look but when he lifted the cover, it was golden brown all over. When I tasted it, it was the best bread I ever ate. I don't know if it was because I was so hungry for bread that it tasted so good, or whether it was because it was baked in the hot sand. I thought if I ever happened to be out in a camp again I would never go without bread if my husband was around. That was something else I learned from him.

Jim's background

I travelled with my father when I was growing up, fishing and tailing rabbit snares. I thought as I watched him build his fires and make his camps ready for the night that he was pretty clever. When I married Jim and started to travel with him I saw that he had a better knowledge of how to build a fire and set up a camp for the night. He was such a lover of nature that he knew just how to handle it. After I watched him a few times and saw how he managed things so well, I never felt afraid with him in a canoe or boat or on dog team. I always felt safe with him, as I have been with him in rough weather and fine and he could always find a way out. I often heard people remarking about how clever he really was. Many people spoke of him as a very fine man.

I learned a lot about Jim's life after I married him. He was a very mature man. At times I would find fault with some people I didn't care about. He would check me and say, "You have no right to talk about anyone." I never heard him back-bite people. He would say, "There is good in every person." I was very young when I married him, only eighteen years old, and Jim was twenty-seven. He was already settled in his life and he was very home-loving. I was young and liked gay life. I liked dancing and visiting friends. Jim thought I ought to stay at home with him. Life was very dull for me at first but I got used to it. It was the custom for the man to run the home, the women took second place. A woman could have her say around the house but about the main things in life, the man always had his say. His word went for most everything. Women accepted this and thought nothing about it. They were not hard men; they were kind. They were not very hard to please, so a woman could sew and cook and look after her family; that was the most that was expected of the wives. Jim always got me a cup of tea after I had all the children put to bed when he was at home.

As August passed by and the flies began to leave, the children could get out and play again. The dogs were out again too. One day I couldn't find Marie. I was looking everywhere for her and finally found her asleep, lying on a dog's neck. It was the leader of the team and he was very quiet. They were both sleeping. I did not know how to go about waking them up. I woke the dog first by speaking to it and calling it by its name. The dog opened its eyes and wagged its tail. I picked up my little girl who was still asleep and took her home, and she never woke up. I was very much relieved. Sometimes, when you wake an Eskimo dog out of its sleep, it acts a bit surly. They growl sometimes so I was afraid to wake the baby first. It turned out all right and no one got hurt.

About August 20 we went back to our winter place. My baby was due in early September. The day we left Tikkle to start home we only had an open motorboat, which was about thirty-five feet long. Shortly after we left, it started to blow. A heavy wind from the east came up. When we got out around the point that faced the ocean the wind was so heavy our boat could not stem it. We had to put into Big Bay for the night with the man we fished for during the summer. There were people there so we spent the night.

Caught in a storm

The next morning we got up early and the wind was coming from the northwest, blowing about twenty miles per hour. We didn't have much food, but the people there didn't want us to go. They thought it was blowing too hard. Jim said we had better try to get to Davis Inlet. There was a fair wind out of the bay, but when we got out to turn up to Davis Inlet we had the wind against us. Just as we turned the point our steering wheel broke. We could not go back as it was blowing too hard. We had nothing to keep the boat straight, only an old boat paddle.

Just after we got the boat straightened out heading for Davis Inlet, we saw a shark behind the boat. There was no time to watch the shark—we had to hope for the best and keep going. It was almost blowing a gale. Jim was busy keeping the engine running and Archie, his brother, was helping him. I was trying to keep the boat straight and trying to watch the shark. He didn't follow us very far. I saw him bite at the paddle. The children were afraid. Horace was crying, but his dad couldn't pay any attention to him, he was too busy with the boat. If we had broken down or lost our steering paddle, we would have been driven out to sea.

We had about two miles of water to cross before we got to land. It took us about two hours to reach close enough to it to put the anchor out. There was about a foot of water in the boat. We were all soaking wet, children and all. We could not get near the land, because the water was too shallow. We had to go on to Davis Inlet.

We were out of the heavy wind and only had to follow the shore. About an hour and a half later we reached Davis Inlet. We got food from the Hudson's Bay Company there. We stayed overnight and got everything dried out and sold our fish the next day. We paid our bills and bought enough to get us through until the trapping season opened.

On August 24 we arrived at our winter place. We had a nice day. We had to go about twenty-five miles up Upitik (Merrifield) Bay to the end of our trip. I had lots of work to do. All our blankets were soaking wet from the storm and all the children's clothes were dirty. I didn't have much time to clean up. My baby was due early in September. I was busy getting ready for it. I washed all my blankets and cleaned my house.

Jim was busy cutting wood and getting our fish dried for the winter. He also picked berries for the winter. I couldn't go. My children were too small, so I had to stay home. Jim didn't stay away at night because we were expecting our baby any day. We couldn't afford to get help to stay at home with me.

Third child born

Just a week after we arrived home from the fishing place the baby arrived. It was the second of September and he was a boy. He weighed nine pounds, seven ounces. His father looked at him. He was proud because it was a boy. While he was looking at him he said, "What are we going to call him?" I told him, "You name him this time." So he said he would call him Robert Bruce. So that was what we named him.

I asked him why he wanted to name him Robert Bruce and he said that he had read a book about Robert the Bruce of Scotland. He had been a great man. Jim had Scottish blood in him. He said that they were good, straightforward people. That was how he felt about them. I joshed with him and said, "You and your Scotchmen!"

For three days after having a baby you weren't allowed

to sit up except to eat meals. We weren't allowed to eat meat for three days, only soup from the meat. We were allowed to eat fish. I didn't think all these rules were necessary, but they were the rules of our people. I respected them and went by them.

As the days passed Jim stayed home with me. We couldn't afford to pay a girl so he took over everything—cooking, laundry and scrubbing the floors. We managed. He was pretty glad when the day came for me to get out of bed. He didn't stay in the house very long after I got up!

I had a lot of things on my mind. I only had a month to get all Jim's boots made and clothes prepared for the trapping season. Again it was a good job for me. My babies were quiet and slept a lot, or I would not have been able to keep up with all my work.

Jim was very busy getting wood for me and making his snowshoes and his sled to haul all his food. He would leave in his canoe but his sled was used to haul his furs home and to bring fresh meat for us to eat.

Soon it was October 10, and it was time for Jim to leave for his trapping lines. Our baby was one month old and everything was well with us. I was left alone for two months with my three children. I didn't have much time to be lonely. I had to do everything from chopping wood to baking bread.

I was picking up my strength again and I could manage quite well. My baby was growing like a top and gained about one-and-a-half pounds in October so he was very healthy. Anyway, we hoped his dad would bring home some furs.

Two months passed quickly but when I would lie down at night, I could not help thinking, suppose Jim had an accident, suppose he drowned or set off the gun, perhaps shooting himself. It was loneliest when I would go to bed at night because everything was quiet. I would not get a letter or hear from him until he got back. That was one of the bad things about being a trapper's wife. I talked to many of my friends and they all had the same story, that long wait without hearing from their husbands. We only had to live in hope that they would come back safely.

In a trapper's life, not many accidents happen; sometimes, they would tell us, they had a narrow escape on the new ice in the fall or running in the swift currents in the rivers. The trappers are very clever men in canoes. I felt just as safe with my husband in a canoe as in a boat.

Life at home, fall 1925

My baby continued to grow and kept well all fall. We had one man and his wife living nearby, so the woman came in and babysat for me about three hours and let me go picking berries. I never could leave my baby very long because I was nursing him.

One thing we had that fall was nice weather. The temperature kept in the thirties and forties above zero. We had very little rain or snow so when December came around, we had it colder. Some nights it would be thirty or forty degrees below zero. We only had wood stoves and no oil heaters. When the fires went out after eleven o'clock it got pretty cold. I always kept a diaper under my pillow to change the baby during the night in winter. My babies slept in a heavy wrapper that covered them right from the shoulders to the feet. The fires were made about six o'clock in the morning. We would have to make about three fires and it would be an hour before the house was warm enough to take the children out of bed. Every night in winter, when it was thirty or forty below zero outside, it was below freezing inside the house. I often got up in the morning and had to break the ice on top of my water bucket. I raised nine babies in winters like that and I never had one get sick from the cold and I had some of my babies in mid-winter.

Our home had one bedroom, a kitchen and a porch. I did not have any furniture other than what my husband made. He made the table and chairs and a couple of benches for the children. Every Labrador home had a special little bench about twelve inches high for nursing our babies on. It was made of special wood, birch or juniper. It was the hardest wood we had. Later on in my life, I saw mothers dressing their babies on the table but I dressed them all on this little bench on my lap. My grandmother's bench was a little round one with six legs on it. They were also used for making the boots for the family. They were just the right size for holding sewing on your lap. This little bench was used a lot for the little children to sit on. Jim was pretty good at working with wood and he built a high chair for the small ones.

As the fall season passed by and winter drew near I would get up in the morning and look around me. The land was beautiful with snow on the hills and the green salted water showing its colour against the white hills. It was beautiful, and about twenty below zero. The salt water does not freeze hard enough to drive a dog team over it until the first of January. It takes about thirty or forty below zero weather to freeze salt water solid. As I looked out over the green water and the white hills, I could not help wondering what winter had in store for us. I looked at our little baby in his cot and forgot my troubles for a while.

January 1926

In January 1926, Jim got home with his first catch of fur. He did very well with furs that time. The winter looked brighter for us and I was very happy for the children. Jim stayed home for two weeks and got wood for us. He went back into the country again for another haul on his traps. He came across a company of caribou and killed four so he brought out two for us. At home, our dog team was very small. We only had three dogs. He only could take two caribou but we had lots of fresh meat for the rest of spring. He went into the country again on the first of March and he came home the middle of April.

While he was gone for the month of March, a big storm came on and we had to stay indoors for a couple of days. The second day, I was running out of water. I would have to walk on snowshoes about ten minutes and haul it on the *kamutik*. About three o'clock I was dressing myself up to go and I heard a faint knock on my door. I stood still for a moment wondering who would be coming on that stormy day. I went to the door and opened it and standing before me was a starving Indian. I looked at him, his clothes were worn and had some holes in them. He was trying to talk to me by making signs with his hands. I looked behind him and his wife was standing there. Her clothing was full of drifted snow and she was trying to tell me something. I looked behind her; there were two children, one about three years and one about five years old. I had to take them in because they couldn't go on to Davis Inlet. They had to go there to get food but the storm was too bad. They were dirty and very thin. The man was the worst.

I had a little corner behind my stove about four by six feet and he asked me if they could have that. I said yes.

We got their bedding in the house and a few belongings they had. I was all dressed up in my boots and dickie[12] to go and haul some water because I was right out. I did not have enough for the night so I went outside and got the barrel on the *kamutik* and put my snowshoes on. He followed me out and saw what I was doing. He put on his snowshoes and helped me to fetch the water. All the time I was digging a hole for the water, he was trying to help and he was trembling. I told him not to bother but he insisted in helping me. We were gone about twenty minutes. When we got back, it was almost dark. I got to work and boiled the kettle and put on a good cup of strong tea. That was all they would take first, so the children and I had our supper.

After we were finished, I asked him if they wanted their supper. He told me not to put much on the table because they would eat too much. He said they could not eat too much because they would hurt their stomachs. He told me to give them a little bread with lots of grease shortening on their bread. He watched his wife and children and when they ate two slices of bread he made them stop. After they ate, they got out the bedding and made up the bed and had a sleep. While they were sleeping, I baked some more bread. I was worried about my children picking up a germ because a lot of Indians at that time were infected with tuberculosis. The house was small and it worried me, but they could not go out in the storm. I hoped they would be able to go on the next day but the storm was just as bad so I knew I had them for another day. I had to make more bread. They were shortening my small supply of food. Jim was not coming home for another week.

The second day I kept all our dishes boiled. I was busy all day trying to keep the children from getting into the corner where the Indians had their few things. As evening came around it was still stormy and we could not see any further than a hundred feet from the door, but I had to get out again and bring in my wood and water. The Indian saw what I was doing so he dressed up and came along and helped me. We got through again for another day. As night came on, the storm got worse. I went out just as it was getting dark to bar all the doors. I looked outside and I am sure I could not see any more than five feet from the door. We were all shut snug in the house for another night.

The next day I got up and looked out; my windows were drifted halfway up. It took me and the Indian all day to dig out our windows and doors. By the evening, the storm was getting better; we could see the tops of the trees on the islands in the bay. It began to look a little brighter. The Indian woman stayed near the fire all day and kept the children from being hurt. After we got all our work done, the Indians were awfully happy and said that they would go to Davis Inlet the next day. He made signs and tried to talk to me and after a while I realized what he said: "I know you haven't got much food." The following day, the storm passed and they started for Davis Inlet. The morning was clear and cold. It was about thirty-five below zero. I watched them lash up their sleds. The woman put the little ones on her sled. She dressed up the five-year-old and put his parka on which was made of fawn deerskin. She tied his snowshoes on his feet and he followed behind their sled. They looked much better than when they came to my house. They had had a good rest.

Jim came home after three or four days and we were almost out of food. Next morning, he headed on to Davis Inlet to get a supply of food. I told him about the Indians and he was glad I took them in.

It was getting well on towards the end of March and Jim had to go back in the country and strike up his traps. While he was away, I was busy getting all our boots made for the spring. The days were longer. We had about twelve hours of sunshine. It looked brighter for me because it wasn't so cold for bringing in the water and wood.

Jim came back April 15 and he had a few furs. He said he would go to Hopedale and sell them. He said, "You and the children can come along too." I was glad because the children and I had been in the bay since October and now it was April. We started for Hopedale. We had six dogs and they were a pretty good team. They were lively and they could travel fast. The next day we got to Big Bay and in three days we got to Hopedale. We stayed four days and then a mild spell came. The snow began to melt and the wind came from the southwest. It was about thirty above zero and the snow was melting fast.

On the fifth day we started back to Big Bay. When we had to cross a bay that evening about four o'clock, the dogs were wading in snow and water right up to their bellies. They could not get any footing in the snow to haul the *kamutik*. There were two other teams with us, the mailman and the HBC servant, Mr. Gilbert Saunders. They all had to walk in water and snow up to their knees and help the dogs. We didn't get to Big Bay until about eight o'clock that night. I was in the coachbox[13] on the *kamutik*. We were all tired and the dogs' feet were sore from soaking in the water all day. They were really tired but it looked like we would get a frost that night. We still had another bay to cross. We got up early in the morning and there was a little frost on the snow. We crossed about two miles of land before we got to the bay. When we got out on the bay, there was enough snow and frost on the ice to keep us from breaking through to the water. We reached Davis Inlet that day. We could not stop. We just stayed for the night and went on. Early the next morning, we reached home at Upitik Bay.

The mild weather set in for about two weeks. The snow all melted to water and we had to wait for it to drain off the ice.

Spring 1926

My baby is eight months old now and he can crawl around the floor; he is a very happy little boy and no bother.[14] I can get on well with my work. It is the month of May now and Jim is gone hunting seals. He went out to the open water. It is about fifty miles from where we live. He saw a few walrus that trip, but did not get one because his rifle was not powerful enough. I wish he had got one because I have never seen a walrus. He got a few other seals and I had to clean the skins and make boots for the family for the rest of the spring. With my baby, I am going to be very busy. It's June now and the ducks are coming in the bay to lay their eggs. We will have lots of ducks to eat and fresh eggs and lots of fresh trout.

We have summer in July and August. The flies, mosquitoes and black flies are plentiful then. I could not put my baby down to sleep without a covering of cheesecloth over his bed. I never had trouble with fly-bite infections. I used to bathe the bites with bread-soda water every night before I put the children to bed. In the morning, all the red infection around the fly bites would be gone.

I tried growing a garden when I was up there but it is only in July and August that you are clear of frost. I sowed on June 15 and went out to Davis Inlet for July and August. I had a few turnips and cabbage when we came back in September but they had grown only about six inches high. They were very strong little plants, not big enough to eat yet but very bushy and clustered together. They were really tasty and nice to eat later on. The turnips grew only to about the size of a small rubber ball. We did not have many that size. We left that summer because Jim got a job with the Hudson's Bay Company in Davis Inlet building a chapel for the Indians. The Company wanted a place for the Indians to worship when their priest came around in the summer.

Jim had a job there for two summers. We managed pretty well for the two summers he was working. We did not have a very good place to live, just a one-room apartment, but we had more comfort in Davis Inlet because the flies were not as bad as they were in the Bay where we lived. That was a relief with a small baby. There were women with children there, too, so we shared our troubles and joys with one another.

I used to make some money myself in the summer. I would do embroidery work for an American doctor. He made a trip up north every summer. He would leave orders for caribou slippers and other souvenirs that he wanted to take back to the States with him. He gave my children their first Christmas tree. It was an artificial one, all decorated with ornaments.

Fall 1926

The summer slipped by quickly. In September we moved to the winter place again but we enjoyed September better than July and August because all the flies were gone and the weather was nice. We had temperatures of fifty-five or sixty-five degrees of heat. We had that all of September. When the weather was dry the wild berries were ripe, so we had plenty of berries to eat. We did not have as many kinds of berries in the north as we did back home at Mud Lake up the Hamilton Inlet. We only had partridge berries, blackberries and bake-apples. Back in Mud Lake, where we came from, we had wild raspberries, red currants, partridge berries, squashberries and marshberries. Marshberries are much like cranberries except they are smaller. They make good jam and they are better picked during spring. As soon as the snow and ice go, you get them from the marsh lands. We also had blueberries. We missed the berries when we moved north, especially the raspberries and red currants which made such good jelly.

We ate plants in the springtime when I was a girl. We used to eat dandelions. We picked them before they bloomed because Mother told us they were not so bitter then. They were strong to the mouth. In order to get rid of that bitter taste, she boiled them in two changes of water. She ran the first water off and in the second water she put a little corned beef and piece of fat back pork. It took about two hours to cook. I did not get a chance to use them for my children because they did not grow north where we lived. We used to eat a willow leaf too in the spring. They are quite like greens. We ate them with molasses and the only name they had was *akuviuks*. It's a name that everybody called them in the north.

It is October now and my baby is one year old. He can walk now and is very proud of himself. On the fifteenth of October Jim was away setting his traps along the bay.

There are signs of foxes so he will trap along the bay until November. He will use his boat and wait to go inland until the river freezes up. The sun is setting and it is only about thirty above zero. I have my fire burning beautifully and I will sit with my children until it is dark enough to light the lamp. Jim will not be home tonight so I will be alone. I will have plenty to do because I will be busy sewing. I have a team of dogs around my door to keep away the wolves and bears so my mind will be at ease. Sometimes the dogs howl in the night and I would wonder what was coming, and it would only be one of the team gone astray and they were howling for it to come back. A team of dogs can be great company when you are alone.

Jim returns from the trapline

On October 16 I looked forward to Jim coming home. Evening came and the sun was setting low. I looked out in the distance and saw him coming. He had a black bear and a seal and some ducks for us to eat. We were busy for a day cleaning them all.

Our team of dogs always went down to the boat to meet my husband when he came home from a trip, greeting him with wagging tails. But that time, they would not go close to the boat. We told our neighbour and he said that it was because there was a black bear in the boat. Jim just laughed thinking it was a joke. Next day when he skinned the bear, he went outside and went among the dogs and they all growled at him. He tried to feed them some of the meat and they would not eat it. Shortly after, he told several other people about it and they all said an Eskimo dog won't eat bear meat unless it is starving. They will eat white bear meat but not black bear meat.

I dreaded the winter coming again because we always had water problems. We had to melt a lot of snow because there was no river nearby and we lived by salt water. There was a little brook which we used in summer but it froze over in winter and dried right up. There was a cliff about half a mile away and the water came out of the ground and ran over the cliff. I would take my kamutik and go and fill a barrel with ice and melt it and use it for drinking water and for doing my laundry which was a daily routine. All the women had to manage like that when their husbands were away on their trapping grounds. The six years I spent in the north were much harder than back at Hamilton Inlet where I came from. We had lots of fresh water back there and I missed that very much.

It is near the end of October now and Jim is away having a round on his traps. He trapped a few fox while he was waiting for the river to freeze up so he could get into the country to trap the inland furs. This is better for me and the children because he is only away for a night. I am busy washing my blankets for the winter while the little brook is still running and I can get lots of water. I did not have much time for pleasure because all the laundry had to be done by hand.

By November it started to get pretty cold. We had a couple of snowfalls and the ice gathered on the shore. I used to look out late at night and there would be a breeze blowing over the salt water. It showed the blue and green shades in the rippling sea tops. I would go outside after supper when I was alone and take a long look at the beautiful northern lights dancing across the sky in their beautiful shades of light yellow, purple and orange. This was all I had for entertainment but I loved it. I often looked at the northern lights for an hour when my children were asleep. Sometimes, during the day I could look out and see a seal or a duck swimming by.

My two eldest children went outside in the daytime. I was sometimes afraid that the dogs might bite them but we had our team for six years and never had a child bitten by them. There was a boss dog in the team and he looked out for the children. The dogs were all I had for company. They always let me know when a boat was coming. They would all go down to the beach and howl so I would know there was a boat close. Sometimes, they could hear it when I could not see it. They would know if it was a strange boat and would come back again to the door. If it was our motorboat, they stayed down on the beach until the men put down the anchor. They would come back to the door and lick my hands and wag their tails as much as to say, "We are glad they are back."

The mad lynx

In the month of February 1927, Jim and Archie were ready to leave for the country. Archie took sick with a bad headache and he could not travel for a week. On February 15 they started. Jim took the dog team and travelled on the river and Archie went to a set of fox traps they had about two miles from the house. They left about eight o'clock in the morning. At one in the afternoon, Archie's wife went to empty a pail of water but came in the house in a hurry and said that she had seen her husband walking along the shore about two miles from the house. She got uneasy and thought his head was bad again and we thought he was wandering around and could not find his way back. Jim had already gone from the house for four hours and he was about five miles up the river.

Since Lily was crippled, the only thing I could do was go and try to find out what had happened. I put on my snowshoes and started. There were only about two hours of sunshine left in the sky so I had to hurry. He was out of sight in the woods again when I left the house. I walked in a hurry and watched for him. At last he came out to the shore again. He saw me and waited. I was about 200 feet from the shore and we were both getting ready to speak to each other when I saw an animal coming behind him. It was grey and Archie heard it at the same time, but before he had any time to do anything it was on his snowshoes. It must have seen me because it came right on after me. In the few moments of confusion, neither of us spoke. Archie took a second look and saw it was a lynx, a wildcat. There was not much time to do anything so he cried out to me to jump. I went in the opposite direction. He was a sure shot with his rifle and the lynx had to stop before he could catch me. Archie fired when it stopped and shot it right through the body. That was all that saved me.

When we met, we were both shaken up over what had happened. It was a little while before we could talk and find out what had happened. I asked him why he was there that time of day, making us worry about him. He said when he got to the set of traps he went to see in the morning, there was a fox taking the bait from the traps. He took a shot at it and broke its leg so he chased it for three hours and he still did not have it. We had the lynx then and I said that I would carry it home. There was about an hour before darkness so Archie went back after the fox. I finally got home and told everyone what had happened.

Just about dark, Archie came and he had the fox too. It was a good fox and a good lynx. About supper time, I began to feel awfully bad. I was trembling and felt sick at my stomach. I was three months with child and Archie's wife thought I was going to lose my baby. That night I could not sleep; I had to walk the floor all night. Jim was about twenty miles up the river wondering what had happened to Archie. Archie had to leave before daybreak to catch Jim before he would start for home.

I stayed quiet for a few days and did not lose the baby. Archie and Jim went on into the country. They did not stay long because Jim was uneasy about me. They killed a couple of caribou and came back in about ten days. When they found I was all right they went right back again. They came out the next time on April 15. They did not get many furs so they cut their wood for the next year.

Seal hunting

In the month of May, Jim and Archie went out to the edge of the ice, right out to the ocean, to hunt seals and white foxes. They were gone about one month. They got a few foxes and seals. When they came back that was the last for the winter so they put away the traps and their *nouluk*. This was a type of harpoon they used for darting the seals. When the seals came up to their breathing holes, the men would dart them with the *nouluks*. It was a tool with a long wooden handle and a piece of iron rod at the end about two feet long. At the end of the rod was a detachable spear point on a long line made from sealskin. This was how they killed the seals, usually late in the month of May.

The next thing to work on was the trout and salmon nets that had to be netted and mended. The month of June was used to make the nets and repair those that were broken. In July, they caught trout and in August, salmon. There was no way to sell fresh fish so we sold it by the barrel in salt to the Hudson's Bay Company. Archie stayed in the bay and salmon-fished. Jim went to Davis Inlet and got a job as a carpenter. I moved out with him because I was expecting my baby in the month of August. Everything went quite well that summer.

A fourth baby is born

I was afraid when my baby was born that it would be deformed in some way or other because I had such a fright with the lynx in the month of February. On August 27, May was born. When the midwife brought her to me I looked at her and she looked more like a lynx than a baby. But it was only her head, her body was all right. Her face was not quite right and her hair was sticking up all over her head. I was so worried about it. She reminded me of the lynx because when I had looked at it coming for me out on the ice, its hair was sticking up all over its head, with two big teeth in front of its wide-open mouth. The next morning when the midwife bathed my baby, I saw there were two teeth sticking out of her gums so I did not know what to expect of her. What if I would have to look at her head with the hair sticking up all her life and perhaps also a mouthful of big teeth?

Treated by Sir Wilfred Grenfell

Three days after May was born, I took very sick for a week. I did not know anything that was happening. They told me after I got better that I was running a very high temperature. We heard Sir Wilfred Grenfell was coming up the coast and the day he came to Davis Inlet, my husband was out in the harbour waiting for him. Jim brought him ashore and when he examined me he said I had infant fever.[15] He went aboard his boat and got me some drugs and some oranges and soda biscuits to eat. He went on further north to visit the coast. Shortly after, I began to feel a little better but I was not well for a long time. That fall, I stayed in bed fifteen days altogether.

I had three other children to look after and my husband had to work every day or lose his job. I had to get out of bed the fifteenth day and try to look after the children. We were staying with Freeman Saunders and his family and his wife Nomi was expecting a baby. She could not help me very much so we were both in a helpless state. I used to get up for a while every day and take care of my baby and feed my children. Then, I would have to go to bed again. September passed by and we went back in the bay to prepare for winter again. I was still sick but I could manage to stay up all day. I had to go to bed early at night.

Baby Bruce is accidentally burned

October passed by and Jim went setting his traps again. The first evening he was gone I was alone cleaning my floor. I looked around for my children. The girl Marie and the second boy Bruce were sitting by the stove watching the fire burning. I checked them to see if everything was all right and went on about my work. About ten minutes later, the whole house lit up with fire. I jumped to my feet and I was by Bruce's side in a minute. I did not know what to do; I saw a big coat close by and caught it and smothered out the flame. For a few seconds, he didn't move. I picked him up and the minute I moved him he went into a "rock of pain." I was a whole hour trying to keep him on my lap. That was between five and six in the evening; at about six-thirty, he fell asleep. Jim was still not home so I laid Bruce on a big wooden chest I had beside the table. I thought I would have something to eat because I expected to be up all night. I looked over his body as carefully as I could and I saw his right arm was burnt right to his body and one cheek, one ear and both his lips were burned, so I knew I had a terrible task on my hands. I tried to eat but couldn't. I walked the floor and the other children were afraid that their little brother would die and they were crying. Their daddy was not home yet.

About seven o'clock I heard the boat coming and I was there with my little boy all burnt. I did not know how his dad would take it. I thought that he might think that I had been careless and got him burnt so I just sat by my little boy and waited for Jim to come into the house. I told him what had happened. We sat beside our child and when he woke up he again went into a rock of pain. We walked the floor with him the whole night taking turns.

He could not even take a drink during the whole night. In the morning, he seemed to be better and asked for a drink. Then he fell asleep so we had a chance to look over his whole body. There were burns on his legs as well as his arm and face. We sat down and tried to figure out what we could do. The only thing we had in the house was a bottle of castor oil. I said to Jim, "You better get me a juniper stick and I will boil it and use the liquid to bathe the burns." I had no dressing. I had a couple of sheets and I tore them up for dressings. There was a small wound of open flesh on his elbow and I was really afraid that would become infected. I hoped and prayed it would be all right. Jim got the juniper stick. I went to work and boiled it four hours and started to bathe the wounds in the liquid.

On the second day, the spot on his elbow looked a bit red and infected. I took a piece of the stick and peeled the outside bark off and took the inside, the gummy bark of the stick, and beat it to a pulp. I sterilized my dressing by browning it on the stove and I placed a piece of the gummy pulp on his elbow. I greased the poultice with the castor oil and after six days he seemed to be getting a lot better.

There was a doctor at Nain with an explorer, Captain MacMillan from the United States. They were stationed at Nain but travelled all the time. MacMillan's doctor travelled to Hopedale and used to travel north to Okak, so we didn't know if he was in Nain or not. After eight days, my husband thought our little boy was better. Jim went out to Davis Inlet and waited for a day. On the second day, the doctor passed through Davis Inlet on his way to Nain.

Jim brought him up the bay the next morning. He looked at our boy and at what I was using and he said he was over the worst. He told me to carry on with what I was using. He gave me some dressings and I was very happy about what he told me. He said I had done a marvelous job so my mind was at ease then.

I was still sick myself from the infant fever and I had lost a lot of weight. The doctor said to me, "You should be in a hospital yourself." I was so frightened when the baby was burned that I hadn't eaten for four or five days. Jim stayed home with me for a month. It was three weeks before I could dress my little boy. I had three other children and the youngest was only two months old. We both worked night and day for about three weeks. With hard work we helped to save our little boy. We were both upset for a week because we did not know what was going to happen. You can't imagine what we went through that fall but the main thing is that we got through and out little boy got well again. Many, many times after, we both wondered how we had done it. But with God's help, we fought for his life together. For three weeks neither of us had a full night's sleep but the main thing was that he lived and we were both very thankful. When two people work so hard together to try to save a child, it is good to see him recover.

As time passed by, Bruce really began to get well again. His appetite came back and he began to go outside with the other children. By the end of November, he was back to normal again.

Jim was waiting for the river to freeze over with ice to get in to his inland trapping lines. He lost most of that fall waiting for Bruce to get well. He got a few foxes and a few seals trapping around the bay. We had lots of wild ducks to eat and also Arctic hare which are bigger than rabbits and much better meat. They live on blueberries and off the shrubs on the side of the high hills. I could make a much more satisfying meal with Arctic hare than I could with the caribou meat.

Christmas 1927

Until December 1927, Jim stayed home waiting for our son to recover. The cold weather came quite early and froze over the river. He made a quick trip into the country and set up his traps and came back for Christmas. We spent our Christmas as a family together, the first one for a long time. It was a very quiet day.

The children hung up their stockings in those days. There were not many gifts. The boys had a rubber ball each and our little girl had a little doll and a few candies that had been saved in the fall for Christmas. There was an old man and his wife living near us and we took the children over to see them in the afternoon. We sang Christmas carols and read the Christmas story. We went home and had a quiet evening by ourselves. This was the way things went at Christmas in Labrador in the bays on the coast. We always visited with one or two families. The Christmas feast was made up of fresh baked partridges or baked rabbits or caribou steaks. The pastries were partridge-berry pies and the cake was made of molasses, raisins, currents, spices and baked in the oven like you bake a plain white bread. This was Christmas in Labrador and we were all quite contented with it.

Financial troubles

In January 1928, Jim went back into the country and had a haul on his traps. He did not get many furs so it did not look so good for us. We had a very cold winter. Jim kept himself busy on his trapping lines. We were getting behind. We were not getting enough furs to keep up with the bills we owed the Hudson's Bay Company. The winter was looking pretty grim.

March came again and the weather was getting a little warmer. The worst of winter was over for another year. On the tenth of March a man named Herbert Decker came to our house. He lived three miles away and his wife's aunt had died. He was looking for help. He wanted me to come and take care of their family while his wife was away helping with the funeral. I got the children ready and took them over to the Decker's. Jim went with Mr. Decker to help dig the grave. The ground was frozen very hard and it took them three days. I stayed with all the children.

Bruce dies

Marie, our little girl, went to Davis Inlet for a trip with her Uncle Arch and Aunt Lily. She came home sick, and three days later my oldest son and the little boy Bruce took sick. Twenty-four hours later Bruce died. I never knew what caused his death so fast. It was a type of sickness with very bad diarrhea, a lot of pain and a high temperature. Jim came home from the Decker funeral the day my little boy took sick. By midnight little Bruce could not recognize us. We were all alone with no help within two or three miles so Jim stayed with me until it was getting daylight and then went for Archie and his wife. Shortly after Jim left, Bruce got worse and kept getting worse. It was bad going for dogs and Jim took a long time. When he got back with help, my little boy was almost dead. When Archie's wife came in the house, she knew how bad it was. She moved Bruce to a table and straightened him out. He was gone in a couple of minutes. Our little boy we had fought so hard to save from burns died a few months later.

We were three miles from the graveyard. We had no place to put the little body. Jim and Archie built a scaffold about six feet from the ground. Jim and Archie and Mr. Decker made a casket for him and put it on the scaffold. The day after Bruce died we started digging the grave. We started out in the early morning. We had to go three miles on dog team to dig the grave and go back home every evening because Horace, our oldest boy, was very sick. We did not know if he was going to pull through or not. Archie's wife was looking after him for me in the day. I went with the men to cook their dinner to give them more time at the grave. The ground was frozen very deep.

It took the men three days to dig the grave. The third day we took the little corpse with us. The only minister around was a long way away. There was an old English gentleman who lived near us who could have buried him for us, but at that time he was in bed with an abscess on his back and could not walk. We took the body into his house and he read a part of the burial ceremony for us. We went on to the grave about three o'clock in the afternoon and Jim and I had to finish burying him ourselves. The two men we had with us could not read and Archie said he could not bury him. We had no other choice but to do it ourselves. It was one of the hardest tasks I did in all my married life.

We went back to Archie's late that evening of the twenty-fifth and our oldest boy Horace was too sick to move. When we pulled up to the door it was after dark and we could hear him crying with pain. Archie's wife told us he was getting worse. We did not know what to expect. We took turns staying up with him all night. About twelve o'clock that night there seemed to be a change in him; his pain was leaving him a little. About three o'clock he fell asleep and at breakfast time he woke up and knew us and called us Daddy and Mommy.

The worst was over and he gradually got better. We had to stay at Archie's for a week until Horace was strong enough to take home. Our home was very lonely without our little boy Bruce. His play things were scattered over the floor just the way he had left them about ten days before. I gathered up all his things and put them away where we could not see them because it made us both lonely.

Jim had to go into the country and put away all his traps for the spring. I was left alone again for a month. I had plenty to do trying to build up Horace and make him strong again. I caught some fresh fish for him and we had lots of fresh caribou. He was not very long getting back his strength. He could get outdoors and play. Everything was looking a bit brighter for us again. But the family chain was broken by the death of our little one. We would go to the table for meals and his place was empty and when we went to bed at night, it was the same thing. We spent a very lonely spring.

Financial troubles worsen

I missed my parents as I had been away from them now for four years. We only got letters from them about twice a winter and about three times in the summer. We were not making money to spare and there was no way of getting home for a trip to see them. Mail was delivered in winter by dog team and in summer by a steamer from St. John's. As each year went by we were a little more in debt. The Hudson's Bay Company was getting a bit more impatient with us.

In 1928, when we went to get our food again for the winter, the Hudson's Bay manager told us that if we could not pay off our bills that year, he would have to cut off our credit. Jim said we would have to do something. We needed a lot of things when our fourth child was born in 1927. We were living in a house in Davis Inlet with another family that summer because Jim had a job with the Hudson's Bay for a little while.

When fall of 1928 came around we went back to the winter place and we thought a lot about it. It was too late to go back to Hamilton Inlet to my father's and his brother's, although we knew we would get a little from there. We stayed on for another winter.

When Jim came out of the country the first time, he did very well with fur. We had to have food to eat and he put all he could against his bills. It was not enough. When he came back, he had his mind made up. He said if he could get enough furs to buy food for us and the dogs, we would get in touch with the mailman and travel down the coast with him because we did not know the way. Archie came to the house one day and Jim told him what we were going to do. Arch said that if we were going back home he was coming too. That was early in 1929. They both went back into the country and they came out March 20. Jim said he thought he had enough furs to buy food for the trip. I had to make a couple of pairs of boots for Jim and boots for the three children and a pair for myself. The trip we had to take was roughly a little over 300 miles by the coast. We both thought it was going to be pretty rough for me and the children but there was not much else we could do because we would not get any help from the Hudson's Bay Company for another winter.

We talked about it and at first I did not approve because I was worried about the children. We would have to go over quite a lot of land. It was up hills and down on the other sides and through valleys. I thought we might cripple our children. We only had six dogs. There were five of us besides our belongings, food and dog food. Jim said he would have to build a new *kamutik*. We had to be ready for the fifteenth of April because the mailman was making his last trip at that time.

3. WINTER DOG-SLED TRIP BACK TO MUD LAKE

Jim built a sixteen-foot *kamutik* and we were ready to leave April 15. We started on a fine morning; the going was good. We loaded up the *kamutik*. The coachbox Jim built for me and the children was about six feet long. It was wider at the top than at the bottom to give me room to hold the children. I had a mattress, which in those days was filled with bird feathers, and a few blankets. The coachbox was covered over with canvas, something like those that were used for a horse and wagon. As we drove over the ice that day, many things passed through my mind. I was sorry to leave my friends behind, but I was looking forward to seeing my family again. We were happy about going home. There were two dog teams as Archie and his family were with us. He had only two children, about twelve and fourteen years old.

Davis Inlet

As we reached Davis Inlet that night the mailman was already there, ready to start next morning. We were to join the next mailman at Makkovik. We started again in the morning. There were four teams of us. The Hudson's Bay servant came as far as Hopedale with us. He went to pick up some groceries for the spring. He had fourteen dogs in his team, the mail team had twelve, we had six and Archie had seven. It took a long time to get all thirty-nine dogs straightened out. The dogs were fighting and the teams were getting mixed up, but we finally got on our way about eight o'clock and made it to Big Bay that day. We were stopped there by a storm for two days.

On the nineteenth we started again and reached Hopedale. The next day was a fine day. It was my twenty-seventh birthday. We travelled on towards Makkovik but it was not a very good day for the dogs. There was a little snowfall and it made the hauling hard for them. We had to stop early that evening at Tikkerasuk. There was only one Eskimo family living there. We all gathered inside and felt that we were imposing on them, but they were very kind and gave us all the room they could spare. We had our own food and food for the dogs. Early in the morning, we left again for Makkovik. We stopped at noon at Ben's Cove and had our dinner at the home of a man named Stanley Evans.

We left Mr. Evans about one o'clock. We wanted to reach Makkovik that evening to catch the mailman from Rigolet. As we travelled on, we had to cross a neck of land called Ben's Cove Neck. After we got across we could see Makkovik in the distance. It was close to sundown and my legs were getting very tired from sitting in the coachbox all day with the children on my feet. We reached Makkovik near dark. It was a Moravian Station. There were a number of families there and a school and church so we all got in a nice home that night. We stayed with Mr. Wilson Anderson and Archie and his family went to Mr. John Anderson's. The mailman went to another home. I got some clothes washed for my children that night and we had a good rest. We left Freeman Saunders, the northern mailman, in Makkovik.

Makkovik

We joined the mailman there from the south, Mr. Steve Noel. He came from Rigolet. We left again the next morning and we had to go over a lot of land that day. It was hilly land with brooks. All the men were dead beat that night from handling the heavy *kamutiks* all day. The children and I got a pretty bad shaking-up that day too. The place we reached that night was called Big Bight, about ten miles south of Makkovik. The name of the people there was Bromfield. We had an east wind that night and a heavy snowfall. We were held up there one more day. I was not sorry because I was tired and I got some clothes washed for the children and baked some more bread. The dogs had a rest from hauling their heavy loads.

After the storm cleared we hit the trail again. We had a long day ahead of us but it was all on ice. We were near a place where a man and his wife had been lost in a big storm the fall before. It was very rough because it was so near the ocean.

We had a great day as we could see the blue ocean and the icebergs beyond us. The snow was heavy for the dogs. Their traces would get all tangled up and the men would have to stop about every second hour and untangle them. The children and I would get out and stretch our legs a bit. We were really enjoying that day.

Sled overturns

Just before we got to Tuchialic we had to go up over a neck of land and over a steep bank. The mailman was ahead of us. He got over the bank all right. We were next. The dogs started up the bank which was about a hundred feet high. They went up all right, but just as they got to

the top, the dogs stopped. The *kamutik* was down over
the bank and it started slipping and Jim could not hold
it. It was too heavily loaded and at last, turned over. The
two eldest children fell out of the box and started rolling
down the bank. Archie was coming behind and he ran and
caught the children before they got hurt. I landed standing on my head in the *kamutik* box with the baby under
my arm trying to keep her from getting smothered in the
bed clothes. By the time I got out, I was almost smothered
myself. After a while, we got everything straightened out
and no one really got hurt.

We drove a couple of miles further before we reached
Tuchialic at about six o'clock. We had been on the trail
that day twelve hours. When we arrived the people were
all out to meet us. The women took the children in and
the men helped our men to unharness the dogs. They took
our load inside and fed the dogs. There were four families
there. We stayed at John Thomas Lucier's. Archie and his
family stayed at Mr. David Edmond's and the mailman
went to Mr. Bromfield's. We all got in for the night. The
people we met there were young people like ourselves.
We had great fun. John Thomas Lucier came home with a
load of fresh caribou and we cooked a big supper. After that
I gave the children a bath and washed their clothes. The
women helped me and I really felt relaxed that evening.
They really were a group of very nice people. I wished the
weather would be stormy next day because I was having
so much fun.

Sore feet

The men were busy all evening repairing dog harnesses
and making dog boots. The dogs' feet were getting sore
from the water on the ice and from hauling every day. The

men greased their feet with seal fat to soften them. When the dogs started to move around some of them had their tails down because their feet were so sore.

The next morning was fine weather so we hit the trail again. We had another nice day. We stopped about noon and had our dinner at a blind woman's home. There were two young people looking after her because her husband was dead. She was making mats out of straw to put under hot plates. She told me she sold them to buy the soap and matches and little things for her house. Her name was Julia Bromfield. The name of the place was Tilt Cove. She was very clean and she was happy. I bought four mats from her and she was awfully glad. We moved on again. We were not travelling very fast because it was too warm for the dogs and their feet were still sore, but we reached Big Brook late in the evening. We met two people from North West River. It was near where my people lived and it was good to see them. We stayed there overnight. The dogs seemed very tired that night, so the men thought we should stop a day and give them a spell. These people had lots of dog food and we gave our dogs a couple of good feeds.

We were ready April 27 and started again. We did not go far before we came to Peter Pottle's. He lived with his mother-in-law who was an old lady sick in bed, paralyzed. We spent an hour with them. While we were there a man named Simon Shuglo came to see how the people were getting along. It was on a Sunday morning. There was a good frost on the snow and the going was good. Simon had a light *kamutik* and he offered to take some of our load. That was wonderful for us. We had to go over land that day called Pottle's Bay Land.

We all got started again with only about two hours' drive to Simon's home. We stopped at his place and had some dinner and then went on again. Simon said he had to make a trip to Rigolet and would come along and help us. We all reached the mailman's home that night. We stayed with Mr. Noel on the twenty-eighth to give the dogs a spell.

Hamilton Inlet

The next day we reached the shores of Hamilton Inlet Bay. We knew the way from there ourselves. Around dinner time we broke away from the other teams and went to visit Jim's brother Albert and sister at Green Point up in Tom Luscomb's Bay. Archie went on to Rigolet with the mailman. We stayed there a day and Albert got ready and came on with us. We had to go about another ninety miles before we reached home at Mud Lake. We did not mind then; we knew our way.

On the first of May, we started up the Hamilton Inlet. We took the winter route and went up Double Mer. Albert only had three dogs but his team was fresh so he was able to keep up with us. The first day we went to Job Oliver's at Pompey's Head in Double Mer. The next day, we went across a neck of land called Shep's Harbour Portage to Valley's Bight. We stayed at Peter Shepard's home that night. Then on to Pearl River where my Aunt Jane and Almer Chaulk lived. It was nice to see them again after six years, but I could not enjoy anything, I was so tired from the trip.

When we got to Pearl River, the snow was all off the ice. Along the coast it had been just like winter. The fifth of May we arrived in North West River. All Jim's brothers were there. We stayed a few days and had a rest until the dogs' feet got heated up and they felt better. We only had one more day to go and we would be at my parents' home.

On May 9 we left for Mud Lake going up across Goose Bay. I was sick when I reached home. After a day's rest, I felt better. The trip had taken us twenty-five days, seventeen days of that travelling. Jim was really tired himself. The children were tired too. Our dogs didn't walk around on the snow for a whole week. They lay on the ground where the snow was gone. Jim checked their feet after we got there and he told me their feet were almost worn to the flesh. Those dogs meant a lot to us because they pulled together so well. When we reached Mud Lake our big coachbox and our sixteen-foot *kamutik* would not be of any use to us. Jim took apart the *kamutik* and made it smaller. Our coachbox was of no use at all in Hamilton Inlet. After a few days, I thought back over my trip and the many friends we met as we came along. Sometimes it was late in the evening when we arrived at a house and not one family ever said no to us. They were very kind and I had many happy memories of my trip.

4. Settled Life in Mud Lake

We hadn't told father how poor we were, but after a couple of weeks, Jim said we would have to tell him. Mother and Father were alone one evening, so we told them. Father felt awfully bad. He did not say very much at the time. The next day he talked it over with my brothers and agreed to take us in for the winter. We were so thankful for that. We had three children and we knew it was going to inconvenience them because we could not keep children quiet all the time. Father was very taken up with our oldest son, Horace, and seemed to enjoy him a lot. He was seven years old. As spring passed by, we tried to make the best we could of it. Father had a big motorboat and lots of seal nets. Jim helped him to get the nets ready for the first of June. He also helped him to cut the next winter's wood. Jim hauled it all home because he had our team of dogs.

The first of June came and the men started setting the seal nets. They had to go about fifteen miles twice a week to haul the nets.[16] Father got about fifteen or twenty seals each haul. I used to clean the sealskins. I cleaned eighteen that spring to get skin enough to make boots for my own family. Father gave me one out of every three I cleaned. It was hard work, but we were thankful to be in his home for the winter.

We managed to find our own food. Jim got a little work with the Grenfell Mission. He built a canoe to sell and a small boat for Father. I did sewing for the Grenfell Mission's Industrial Shop and managed to get some clothes for my children. As summer passed by, we managed to keep ourselves alive. Towards fall, Jim got in touch with his brother Fred who told him there was plenty of ground above the Hamilton Falls to make a trapping place. Jim went to see the Hudson's Bay Company and they agreed to let him have a supply of food for three months for the family and himself. We were thankful for that. The men who trapped above the Hamilton Falls had to leave early, around the tenth of September. There were about ten trappers who went above the falls.

I was expecting my fifth child and Jim was a bit worried about me but I kept well all fall. I again took work for the Industrial Shop at the Grenfell Mission and helped to buy milk for the children because we could not get all the food we needed. I was busy all fall and the time soon passed by. I used to set snares and catch rabbits. My mother could not get very far to catch trout so I used to go trouting through the ice and catch enough to eat. Christmas came around and I knew Jim would be home about the twentieth of January. We did not get any mail from him until the first trappers came home and that was only about two weeks before he got home. I got a letter from him brought by my two brothers. They trapped in my father's place in the Valley of the Hamilton River. The letter said that Jim was well and was doing pretty well with furs. I was anxious to know how well he was doing. On the eighth of January some of the trappers came out from near the Hamilton Falls and brought the news that the inland trappers were on their way out and Jim was among them.

They reached Mud Lake on January 20, 1930. We had supper and father said to Jim, "Show us your furs, boy!" So Jim got out his furs and showed them to us. A trapper never tells about his furs until after he comes home. He started to bring in bags of furs. There were four and I knew that they held quite a lot of fur. I was so happy and excited but I didn't say anything. He started to take out the furs and when they were all out, father checked them. My brothers had their furs sold and were back from North West River. They said Jim should get about $800 for his furs. After the boys came back from selling their furs, the Hudson's Bay got a telegram from their head office saying that the fur price had gone up. Jim stayed home for a few days, cleaned up his furs and then went to North West River. There were two trading companies there, the French Company, Revillon Frères, and the Hudson's Bay Company. They both made a bid on Jim's furs. The Hudson's Bay Company bid the highest. When Jim came back he had $1,000.

I was speechless and too glad to be able to sleep that night. I was expecting my baby in February. We were both so happy; we knew we had a start and we would be able to get a house that summer. That would mean an awful lot to us with another baby soon coming. That was really the first break we had in seven years in the way of money.

Fifth child born

Our baby was born on February 18, 1930. She weighed nine pounds and a few ounces. The morning she was born it was fine weather, but cold, thirty-five below zero. The United Church minister in Mud Lake, Reverend Walsh, was leaving for his long trip south. Father went to his house and told him the baby was born, so he could tell the folks as he passed by North West River. Reverend Walsh travelled south as far as Sandy Hill. There was only one minister for the whole coast, about 300 miles. He had calls to make all the way. This was the only visit the church would make for the winter. He would have to perform marriages, baptize babies and bury the dead. It took him a long time. Some of the homes were not very warm and some people were very poor. Our ministers who travelled the coast went through a great deal of hardship. Reverend Walsh made his trip and got back in six weeks and then we had the baby baptized. We named her Isabel Grace.

House building

Jim went back up the Hamilton River for two months. He trapped in my father's place. It was too far to go back to his own trapping place for two months. In April he came back again. He got ready to build a house that summer. He cut all our winter wood and brought it back, then he picked out a place to build our house and he cleared the land. By the first of June, we were ready to start building the house. He bought a second-hand house that the Dickey Lumber Company had left in Mud Lake. We got it for $100. Jim had to dismantle and rebuild it. By the time we got it ready to build again, it was almost the last of July. We only had a little over a month to build it. It is not pleasant working in July with the mosquitoes and black flies but we needed our house. I had two young brothers who gave us some help. By the end of July we had it down and moved to the new location. Jim started to build it the first of August. By the end of August he had it up ready for the roofing and the windows. He had to work day and night almost to get it finished enough to move into before the tenth of September when he had to leave for his trapping grounds. We moved in on the sixth, but he had to leave everything then and get ready for his trip. He had to make paddles and a pole for the rough water. I had no beds and no dish cupboards and no porch. I had to build them myself. Horace, our oldest boy, could help a little; he was eight years old then. He could hold the lumber for me while I put it together. We kept working all fall and we had our beds, the cupboards and a porch. By the time the snow came we had it built.

The reason the men had to leave so early was to get over the Hamilton Falls lakes and lands before they froze up. On the tenth of September the trappers came up from North West River and joined the trappers at Mud Lake. They hired my father and his boat to take them to the Muskrat Falls, twenty miles up the Hamilton River. There was a northwest wind blowing and their canoes were loaded too heavily to travel. On September 11 they left—six canoes and twelve men. It was always sad to see them leave. I had four children and my baby was only seven months old. I was not very far from my father's so I did not feel as lonely as I did when I was up north.

As the fall passed, I had plenty to do. I had all my wood cut and split ready to pile in the woodshed. Horace and I got that in the woodshed before the snow came. We used to burn about ten cords of wood from September to April. That was a lot of wood to pile into the shed. By Christmas I had my house all papered up and my beds built and my cupboards made, so everything was in pretty good shape. When Jim came home he was quite pleased when he saw what I had done. The children were happy; they liked the place where we built the house.

Jim had not done as well with furs as the winter before but we managed to pay off our bills and had some money to spare. Things were beginning to look better for us. We had our own home. We were living near fresh water so I was through melting snow and hauling water. That was a great relief for me so we were all much happier. Although I had enjoyed my stay up north, I could see that life was going to be a bit easier for me. I was doing extra sewing for the Grenfell Mission. We had the choice of taking money or second-hand clothes for our work, so I clothed my children that way.

Our oldest boy, Horace, started school that year. There was a little school in Mud Lake heated by wood. In the mornings the children would have to take two or three pieces of wood in their arms to start the morning fires. The men at the village would keep a stock of wood for the day. Horace and Marie both went to school for a while. Horace was only eleven years old when he started going out into the country on his trapping lines. He only had about three years of school. Marie was kept in school longer.

Horace goes trapping for the first time

Jim was in his fifties then. Horace wanted to go with his father so much that I let him go that spring. He would go to school in the fall and go into the country in the spring with his father. We could not keep him home, he always wanted to be with his father. Jim was beginning to find the work hard and Horace could help him with camping in the evening. He was good company for him so I never tried to keep him home after that. I saw what he meant to his father, as Horace grew older. When Horace could stand the hard work, he went with him all year round.

Sixth baby born

In 1932 I was expecting another baby. As Jim left for the country, he asked me when the baby would be born. I said, "You needn't worry, it is not due before January 18." He said he would be home between the tenth and fifteenth. I kept well all fall. I had Jim's widowed sister with me; she was a great help. On New Year's Eve I discovered late in the afternoon that I was out of lamp oil. We burned coal oil in our lamps. I had to walk half a mile to get to the nearest store which was a sub-post of the Hudson's Bay Company. We had a snowfall and the walking was not very good. I put on my snowshoes and started off with a two-gallon can. I had no trouble going to the store with the empty can but when I started back, I had two gallons of oil. It was almost getting dark by the time I started home. I was in a hurry and before I reached home my back gave out. I had to leave my can of oil. I started on without the can and managed to reach a neighbour's house. She sent her twelve-year-old boy back to fetch the oil. I went home and it was dark then so we had to sit in darkness until he came with the oil. My back was pretty sore and Aunt Bella, Jim's sister, was worried about me. When I got up in the morning, I felt better. Two days later my baby was born. Everything went all right. The baby was our third son and we named him Bill.

This was the second year we were in our house. Jim got some furs but they were not too good. We managed all right and I took it as easy as I could for a while because I had Jim's sister to help me. It was the first time I had had any help when my children were born. As winter moved on and spring came, Jim bought me a 22 rifle. I used to go hunting and fishing. I learned to shoot quite well with my gun. When the partridges were at close range, I could hit just about every one. My next-door neighbour, Mrs. Carl Hope, was a hunter also and we went hunting together. We lived near each other for fifteen years. We did a lot of fishing and hunting together.

We had gardens in the summer. We grew potatoes, cabbage, carrots, beets and turnips. We bought our plants from the Grenfell Mission where they were grown in a greenhouse. One year I had good cabbage; a few weighed eight pounds. As the years moved on, we did a lot better for ourselves. Our garden in the summer helped a lot. While Jim's sister lived with me, I could get out more. She was an elderly lady and I could trust her with the children. Things were much easier for me at Mud Lake. In the summer there was a hay field near our door. Mrs. Hope, our children and I would cut it and dry it for the Grenfell Mission. They bought the hay from us for their cattle, pigs and hens. It was not a very big field. It was what the Dickey Lumber Company left there. My children and I cut and dried about a thousand pounds and I bought clothes for the children from the sale of the hay. Mrs. Hope could cut more because her children were older. We spent the month of August cutting hay with a scythe.

The yearly round

We also picked berries in August and made up jams and jellies. The variety of berries included red currant, wild raspberry and squashberry. They grew up on high willows and made very good jelly. In September we took our children in a rowboat and went about nine miles to pick berries for the winter. We picked them by the barrel.

About four or five women and their children went and we camped out for a week. Sometimes there would be a couple of elderly men among us to help to haul up the boats in stormy weather. There were also a few boys among us. We carried our small children into the berry banks and the ones big enough to walk would follow behind. We took our lunch with us and stayed all day. The berry-picking trip took care of the month of September.

In October we would prepare for winter. We dried our potatoes and cleaned the berries and put them away in a barrel so we would not have to do it when they were frozen in the winter. We washed up all the blankets and piled our wood in the shed. In November it was always colder, ice would be forming on the river shores and the lakes. I did a lot of sewing in November because I could not get around as easily. In December we were always busy getting ready for Christmas, knitting and getting things made up for the children. By January, we were looking for our men to come back from the country. Everyone would take it kind of easy in February. Our men would be home. It was the month for a rest from their first trip in the country. March was the month for catching rabbits and hunting partridges. April was the month for fishing trout mostly. During May, we were fishing smelts for fertilizer for our potatoes and gardens. May was also spent getting ready for seal net-fishing and for hunting wild ducks and geese.

In June, we netted seals. July and August were used for bringing home our winter wood and building the trappers' canoes. Our months were not wasted and we had little time for reading or any kind of pleasure.

Around 1932 for two or three winters, we had very cold weather. It was almost unbearable for my five children and our house was not very warm. I had to keep fires in our stoves all night at times. The nights when it was not so cold I went to bed at midnight and was up to make the first fire at six o'clock in the morning. I had to make three fires before I could get the children out of bed. It was forty and forty-five below zero and I often had to break the ice in the bucket in the house before I could put water in my kettle. I could not bathe my small baby before ten o'clock. Temperatures of twenty below zero were not considered too bad. It kept down to twenty below nearly all January and February. We would manage to keep the house fairly warm at only twenty below. Jim's face was marked by frostbite nearly all winter.

Shopping trip to North West River

One day in late January 1933, Jim came out of the country in late January. He and Horace went to North West River to sell their fur. It was a real cold day but they had a fair wind going down. Jim had told me to look for them back the third day. The third day was very cold and they would have a heavy wind against them. They had no dogs and they were hauling a heavy load of groceries. I started looking for them around five o'clock. It was dark then. I just had my wood and water in for the night. I went inside and kept a good warm fire going to keep the house warm if they should come. I kept looking and listening for them. I kept their supper warm but at last it was nine o'clock and still no sign of them. I said to myself they can't be coming tonight. I took the supper off the stove and got the children ready for bed. It was about forty below zero. I went outside to listen for them, but I could not stay out long, it was too cold. I tried to ease my mind and said to myself that they could not have started back at all that day. I had intended to keep fires all night. I was lying in my bed around eleven o'clock and I heard something making a noise at the door. I went out and there were Jim and Horace and they were thawing their frozen faces with snow before they came in the house. I looked at their feet and they were a cake of ice up to their knees. I thought their feet must be frozen. When they came in the house, I asked what happened.

Jim said that they had a heavy load and it took them a long time to cross Goose Bay. Just when they got into the mouth of the Hamilton River they ran into water under the snow and got their feet drenched in snow and water. They had to hurry and knock all the snow and water off their feet before they froze. The loaded sled was in the water too and they hurried to pull it on the shore. By that time it was too heavy with ice to haul. They had to leave the sled with all the groceries and start for home before their feet froze. They walked fast to keep from freezing their feet, but they froze their faces. They had two miles to walk before they reached home. Jim was worried about Horace because he was only thirteen years old then. They had to stop three times in the two miles and thaw their faces with snow before they got home.

Horace was awfully tired. I was about ten minutes getting his foot gear off his feet. I was afraid to look at his feet, but it was too cold for the water to go through to their feet. Jim was worried about the sled because all our groceries were on it. I got supper and they ate. They were exhausted. The next morning it was still cold but the wind was calm. Their faces were swollen from the frostbite. They had to go back for their sled and get all the ice and snow off it before they could haul it home. They got back in the afternoon and everything was all right except for the evaporated milk. It was frozen solid. We could not afford to throw it away so I got a big tub of cold water and thawed it. It was not too bad. We used it in our tea and coffee. Jim and Horace had to stay indoors for a day or two and let their faces heal a bit. I was tired myself from trying to keep the house warm late at night.

It was the last day of January 1933. I looked at my son that night and thought, he will have to go through the same hard life as his father. All the trappers' wives in the Hamilton Inlet area had trouble with their husbands and sons. Hamilton Inlet is a fresh-water place. Fresh-water frost in the air pierces the skin very quickly. When it is blowing you don't have to go far in forty below zero weather before you are frozen. Our men and boys had to work in all kinds of weather to keep the ball rolling. When the winters were over we were just about exhausted, but we always managed to pull through some way. We were so glad to see spring again.

Blood poisoning

In 1934 Jim said he would try to build another trapping place nearer home. He was beginning to find the trip up and down the Hamilton River too hard. Horace was in his fourteenth year and soon he could take over his father's place on the Hamilton. So the next year they went down Kenamu River on the south side of Hamilton Inlet, near the Mealy Mountains. In 1936 they left the last of February and had a round on the traps, but there were no furs. They came back out of the country near the river where Jim was intending to build a cabin. They started to cut the logs for the cabin and had only cut three or four when Jim chopped his ankle. It was a bad cut and bled a lot. He did not have any sterilized dressing to put on it. He lost so much blood that he got weak and had to stay in the camp. On the third day he got really sick and he took the dressing off his leg. There was a black stripe above his knee.

Jim told Horace to get word to the next trapper as quickly as possible. Horace wrote a letter that night and got up early in the morning and got wood for his dad and told him not to go outdoors while he was away. He walked about four hours before reaching the first trapper's place. He left the letter and went back to his father as fast as he could. When he reached the camp, his dad was outdoors and his foot was bleeding again. He was in a delirious state. Horace was getting pretty tired when the trappers came. He was very young, not quite fifteen. The trappers had nothing to treat the wound, and when they saw the state Jim was in they didn't think he would live to get home.

They asked him that night what he wanted to do. He said to try to get him home if they could. They did not have food enough to stay with him. They got everything ready that night. He was getting worse by the hour. They did not have time to make a proper *kamutik* to haul him on and had to take him on a flat sled.[17] Just after they left Kenamu River, bad weather set in and it stayed bad all the way out. Jim would yell with pain when they had to go up the hills. They tried to be careful but they had to go over hills and cross brooks and through valleys. They would camp early because someone had to stay up all night with Jim. The three men stayed up with him one at a time. They let Horace sleep at night because he and his dog hauled their sled every day. They travelled like that for twenty days.

They finally reached Mud Lake. The children and I did not know anything. In fact, I was not looking for him for another two weeks. The last of March, late in the afternoon, a knock came to my door. It was Mrs. Maud Best. They sent her on to let me know so it would not be such a shock to me as I was seven months with child. Mrs. Best stayed and helped me with Jim when they brought him to the house. I just looked at him and I said to myself that he would never live to see another day. Mrs. Best helped me to clean Jim up and when we undressed him and looked at the foot and leg, there were two abscesses, one on his left leg above the knee and one up in his groin. After we got his wound dressed, we tried to put him to bed but he could not lie down We did not like to disturb him too much, he was so awfully sick.

We got some chairs and fixed him up the best we could. The trappers were already gone. They were all tired out. I turned to Horace and he looked so tired and worn out. He said to me, "Do you think Dad will live?" and I had to say that I did not think there was much hope. He said they worked so hard to try and get him home. It was pitiful to see a boy only fifteen years old with so much worry and concern. We talked about the trip out and the hard time they had. I got his supper and got him a bath and then he went to bed. Then I went to Jim again and I thought he looked worse. He had an awful lot of pain. As the evening came on, he seemed to be getting weaker by the hour. At nine o'clock I sent for my father. He came and stayed with us all night. Father said he did not think Jim would live till morning. I went upstairs to Horace who was sound asleep and I thought I should wake him. But when I looked at Jim again, he seemed to be resting. Father said he thought he was over that bad turn. As morning came on, he looked a little better.

We had no doctor that year in North West River, but there was a nurse. Early in the morning we sent a dog team for the nurse. Herbert Michelin left early and had to go eighteen miles. He had a good team of dogs. When it was daylight the three trappers came to the house to see if Jim was still alive. I asked them all about him and they said he hadn't eaten a meal in twenty days. He used to drink a little warm tea in the evening when they stopped to camp. They told me he never had a bowel movement. I had a bowel syringe and I got two of the men from the neighbourhood to help me. We cleaned out his bowels. After I had that done, he seemed to get a little better. He could not lie down and I noticed a big red sore on his back. We took a good look and realized it was another abscess rising. So we laid him on his side and he fell asleep. He seemed a little better when he woke up. Horace was up then and I asked him if they had any fur. He said no, that they had gone in and set their traps and they came back to build the tilt. His father cut his ankle and they never got back on the traps again. They had to leave everything and try to get him out of the country. When Jim woke up I spoke to him and he recognized me. He said, "Is that you, Mom?" I said, "Yes," and he said, "I knew God would bring me home to you and the children." It made me wonder if it had been his faith that kept him going.

It was getting towards evening and we were looking for the nurse. She came about six o'clock. I asked her if she thought he would live. She said she could not really tell me because he was a very sick man. She looked at the abscess on his back and said she couldn't do anything with it for a few days. She did what she could for him and stayed with us that night. The next morning she took him to North West River Hospital. I didn't hear about him for a few days but when I did, he was still alive. I received a letter from the nurse in about a week and she said the abscess on his back was just about ripe. She said the only chance was to operate. She wanted my consent because he was so weak she thought he might not pull through. I sent her word that if there was any chance of saving his life to go ahead and operate. About a week later, I heard he was improving a little. The nurse wanted me to come to North West River for the spring because I was eight months with child.

It was about the middle of April 1936 and I had to get Horace ready to go back into the country with the trappers. It was getting late and they had to hurry to get back before the river broke up for the spring. After they were gone I sent word to North West River and tried to get a place to stay for the spring. Jim's brother Archie said he would take us for a while, so about the twentieth of April I got a team to take me to North West River. Horace was in the country then and I hoped he would do well with his furs. We would have a very hard spring if he did not. Horace came home around the end of April. He only had two or three furs. I knew we were in for a hard time. Jim was still in bad shape and Horace was too young to do very much. He could hunt a few ducks for our food but I still had to go to the Government. They gave only six cents a day per person.

Hard times

We got flour, tea, molasses, a few pounds of butter and a few pounds of dried beans and peas. The children didn't have much to eat that spring. When Horace sold the few furs he had, I bought a few tins of milk and some rolled oats for their breakfast and managed to save five dollars for the midwife when she delivered my baby. There was an epidemic of whooping cough in North West River that spring and my five children came down with it. One of my girls was very sick. The poor nurse was almost out of her mind trying to lend a hand to everybody. She was worn out. The Grenfell Mission's boarding school took in the school children. There were only two or three children who died of it but everyone in North West River came down with whooping cough.

I had to leave Archie's place because his wife Lily was asked to look after a young woman who was having her first baby—Lily was the best midwife around. So I moved in with Jim's sister who only had a small house with one little bedroom.

Seventh baby

A few days later my seventh baby arrived—May 30, 1937. She got whooping cough ten days after she was born and died seven days later, so along with everything else I lost my baby.

We only had a camp stove but we managed to cook some things on it. It was three weeks before I could do any work because we were up with my sick baby night and day and the other five children were just recovering. It was a hard experience, but with the help of God we got through. Jim was getting over the blood poisoning and his memory was just about back to normal, so after our baby was buried we moved back to Mud Lake. Our six-year-old girl was so weak from whooping cough she couldn't walk and had to crawl about.

In Mud Lake I got strong enough to do my work

and cook for the children, and Jim began getting his strength and his appetite back. He improved enough over the summer to be able to go into the country the first of October. We had quite a struggle to get through that summer. Jim had always cut a thousand turns[18] of wood for the Grenfell Mission every spring to help us out with money, but he was so sick he couldn't do it that year, and Horace was sick, too. They managed to cut enough wood for our own use. Summer passed and in the fall they went down the Kenamu River again and finished the tilt Jim had been working on when he had the accident the year before.

As the fall came on they went about setting a net to catch fish for bait for their traps and saw to it that all their traps were ready to use. They were living on fresh partridge and porcupine and fresh fish and that was the best anyone could get. They kept at it all fall and got home in January. They had some furs and Jim was looking very well after the terrible experience he had gone through. Horace seemed to have grown taller and he was happy. They always brought out a load of fresh meat when they came home which pleased me because it was too cold for me to hunt and fish in the middle of winter. When the men trapped along the Kenamu River it was better for me and the children as they didn't have to leave so early in the fall and they came back earlier in January.

A trip to the trapline

As the year passed we were lucky not to have any sickness in the family and were able to carry on with our work normally. My oldest girl was thirteen then and was a great help to me. Jim's sister was staying with us so I went on a trip with Jim in the spring. Always on his last trip he had to strike up his traps.

We had to go four tilts distance—roughly fifty miles one way. The first tilt wasn't very far so we made it quite early. I walked ahead of Jim all day and broke the trail. I was pretty tired in the evening but I was ready to start again the next morning. That day was a full day's walk to the next tilt. We had mild weather so the snow was wet and it was heavy walking with snowshoes. We walked from eight in the morning until six in the evening. I was really tired that night. I had never undertaken a trip like that before though I had done a lot of fishing and hunting around home. Jim asked me if I could make the four tilts distance. I said, "I'm going to try." I just made it to the second tilt and told him, "I'm too tired to cook supper." We had fresh porcupine. Jim singed it over the fire and scraped it nice and brown. They have a very nice taste cooked this way. Some people skin them but I like them singed. They also make a nice gravy.

Jim was busy putting away our things. He made a fire for me. I rested a while and then he got the wood for the night and I piled it in the tilt for him. He laughed at me because I was so tired but I didn't mind that. He was really good to me. When we were finished gathering our wood, he came inside and took off his wet shoes and made a good fire and put the porcupine on the stove. We lay back on the bunk and fell asleep and when we woke up the fire was burnt out. It was about nine o'clock when we got our supper that night.

The morning of the third day we started early. When I got outdoors I could see the Hamilton River to the west of us and the upper part of the Mealy Mountains to the south. It was a nice sunny day in April and the scenery was beautiful. I was really enjoying myself. We walked all day again, but it was all level land so it wasn't so hard. We saw a few mink, lynx and marten tracks in the snow and shot a few partridges for our supper at the fourth tilt that day. Jim was fixing his traps all day to try and get some fur.

Before going back we went on into the country and came back to the fourth tilt again for the night. It was better coming back because the trail was already broken. The sixth day we started for home. We had a lynx in our trap that day. At the third tilt we went back to the top of the hill and the next morning we started down. We had a mink just after we left the top of the hill. In our other traps we had a lynx, a fox and a mink. We were nearly all the day going down the hill. At the bottom Jim had an otter trap set in a little brook and we had an otter in it. The next day, we got home and caught another mink on the way.

The children were very glad to see us. Everything was fine at home. That was the first time I had left my family to take a trip like that. My face was awfully sore from the sun and my legs were pretty tired too. Jim took a few days spell before going to North West River to sell our fur. Then he went cutting wood for the next year.

The furs were a very good price that spring. The Hudson's Bay manager told Jim he had better buy flour, butter and tea because he was going to be short of these three items if the boat didn't get in by the first of June. Jim bought all the groceries he could and we managed until the first of June.

We couldn't ever trust the boat getting in on time because the coast was often jammed with ice. This worried me all spring because we had six children and Horace was a pretty hearty eater then. He was busy out with his father every day cutting wood. They cut a thousand turns for us and a thousand for the Grenfell Mission. It was the middle of May and the ice was beginning to break up around the shore. The wild birds were coming back for the summer—ducks and geese. We were very glad to see them because our food was getting low. Jim was finishing the mission wood and hunting ducks and I would fish whenever I had a spare day, but I was very busy making boots for the family. Horace got up at two in the morning and hunted birds before he went cutting wood. There was very little open water and there were many hunters because everybody needed food.

There were sixteen families in Mud Lake then and we were all running short of flour. A few men got together and went to North West River looking for more flour but everybody was short there too. The only thing they could get was cattle meal and whole wheat grains from the Grenfell Mission. We had to try to make bread with that. By the last of May we had no butter, tea or flour. The ice in the bay and river wasn't completely broken up for the spring. We moved across Hamilton River to make more space for the canoes because everyone was hunting. That was the only way we could all get a share. Jim and Horace would hunt early and late. Sometimes the children and I were left in camp until midnight.

Jim and Horace went over to John Groves' store which carried a small stock of groceries, mostly for the Indians. Jim thought he might have some tea or butter. Jim got through the ice and found John Groves had nothing— only a little shortening, which was better than no grease at all. The day they went to Groves' they killed a Canada goose and a shell bird. Shell birds are not very good eating because they taste very fishy. I had bread rising to bake that I had made from the cattle meal and whole wheat which I ground in my coffee grinder. Jim and Horace left again in the morning to hunt more birds. While they were away I cooked the shell bird for our dinner and kept the goose for their return. I fried some of the bread dough in a little grease to eat with it. It wasn't very good.

We went back to Mud Lake for the weekend and heard the boat was still jammed in ice up around St. Anthony. It was the first of June and the ducks were moving inland to lay their eggs. We had to start eating seal meat then. The children were the worst off. Everybody shared everything they had until it was all gone. The second week in June the boat was still in ice. Uncle Donald Michelin said he would go to North West River and try to get a little flour. He went and got one barrel, 198 pounds, to divide between everyone in Mud Lake. I had to go up in the morning to get my share before I could give the children their breakfast. He gave about ten pounds to a family and said that if there was any left it would be divided between the families with the most children.

The second week in June we heard that the supply boat was out of the ice but it would take another week to reach North West River. I was cooking a pot of seal meat every day to keep Jim and me alive. The children were so tired of the meat we could hardly get them to eat any. They would eat fish but not meat. There was one family waiting to go to their summer place for salmon fishing and they had to leave. All they had was a pot of cooked seal meat for their nine children, but when they reached North West River everybody shared a little flour with them so they could get on their way. There was no one who really starved but some of us were pretty close to it.

When the boat reached North West River every man who had a boat was there waiting for the anchor to drop and the boat to start unloading. The Indians were on the wharf too, and they started to roll the barrels of flour into the store. Some of them broke the barrel heads in and started taking flour home to their families. I don't know if the Hudson's Bay Company got a count on all these barrels of flour. Nobody really minded if they did or not because they should have had enough to put us through the year. They knew how many people they were responsible for. I wouldn't like to have to go through that again.

When the men got home with the flour the women got out their bread pans and started making bread. For two or three days everybody had a big *mukkoshan*,[19] eating and rejoicing that nobody had starved. Everybody got back to normal again after we got enough food to eat with everyone busy about their summer jobs. That was in 1938.

We had a very hot summer that year. Sometimes it was ninety degrees and we had a lot of dry weather. At last August came and the children and I started cutting hay for the mission and Jim and Horace started bringing the winter wood home.

September came around and I was busy making boots for the men to go back into the country again. My friend Hannah Best and I took our children to pick berries for the winter. We carried the small children on our backs. It was a nice kind of change for us to be away from home. When we went back to the camp in the evening the children were always ready for supper. We cooked it and put the children to bed, but they laughed and played until they got sleepy. We women chatted and did our knitting. We had a lot of fun out of it. The children woke up in the morning ready to go again. Hannah and I were good friends but I lost her a couple of years later when she died in childbirth, the baby too. Her girls live near me now and they look to me often as a friend.

September went by and October was cold, especially in the mornings when we took the trout out of our nets. There would be new ice in the marsh. We had to get the trout out of our nets or the gulls would have spoiled them. We kept our nets out until about the last of October when the ice in the water made it too hard on the hands. About two weeks later we began to fish through the ice.

There were always odd jobs to be done. We went to our rabbit snares and took the birch rind off the trees to light our fires in the morning. There was no such thing as using oil for lighting fires because we had to save that for the lamps. We also had to knit all the stockings for our children on the long winter nights.

Eighth baby

In 1939 everything was going pretty well with no illness. The furs were not too plentiful but we managed all right. I was expecting another baby. Another boy was born April 4. He weighed over eleven-and-a-half pounds. His Grandpa Joseph Blake came to see him and he asked me what I was going to call him. I was intending to call him Joseph after his grandfather, but when he looked at him and saw his big hands he said I better call him Joe Louis. He was the champion then but I ended up calling him Denzil Joseph.[20] He was the largest of all my children and grew fast and was a very healthy baby.

The only work Jim could get that summer was bringing out the trappers' canoes from up the Hamilton River, a very long, hard job. Horace went with him. He was sixteen years old then. Jim really didn't know how many canoes they would be able to bring out so they left July 25. They went up the Hamilton River on into the Height of Land and started to pick up the canoes. They couldn't go in one straight line south because the different trapping places were scattered about all over. After they got on the trapping lines they covered an area of about seventy-five square miles which took six weeks. The trip in all covered about 700 miles.

While they were on the big portage at Grand Falls they met two families of starving Indians. Jim gave them all he could spare—they still had to travel about a hundred miles to get home. Jim and Horace started back with all their canoes. They had some food but there were eleven canoes to bring over the Big Hill portage. They got part of the way back and ran out of food. They couldn't leave the canoes because they had promised to bring them back. So they lived on wild raspberries for three days until they got to the valley of the river. They knew there was a trapper building a cabin at the foot of the big hill. The trapper had gone home but he left some food for them. They were all right then. They still had about seventy-five miles to go but the current of the river was with them. They ran most of the rapids and got all the canoes home but one small one that swamped in one of the rapids. They arrived the fifth of September.

Horace went back up the river that year without his father. He went up part of the way with his Uncle Walter Blake, but that was his first year trapping alone. His dad and I were worried about him a little. We were glad when the time came for him to come home. He did quite well with fur that winter and we were very proud of him. He was only sixteen years old. He went alone every year after that. His father trapped in Kenamu River. Life looked brighter for us then with the two of them able to trap. I was very proud of Horace, my first son.

Marie, our oldest girl, was able to do a lot to help me then. I had more freedom and was beginning to enjoy life more after all the years of hard work bringing up the children.

We had a little church in Mud Lake and had services once a month. I went to the church meetings and took part in the work of the church. We had only one minister to cover North West River and Mud Lake and he had to travel down the coast as well. His name was Dr. Lester L. Burry. He spent twenty-six years in this part of Labrador and baptized four of my children.

The women of Mud Lake met once a week. We had Bible reading and a prayer and then we had a sewing class to raise money for the church. We made dresses and children's clothing. Wednesday of one week we would meet to cut out all the material, then the next week we gave out the work to our women. We worked like that all through the winter. We only had one radio in Mud Lake at that time and it was placed in the school for the teacher but we were allowed to go in and listen to it after school. The war was on then and everyone wanted to hear the war news.

Dr. Burry had a radio outfit to send messages to the trappers and people along the coast of Labrador. He went on the air every night and broadcast church services on Sunday and at last a few people got radios. My father got one and we could go and listen to church services on

Sunday. The transmitter opened up a new life for the people of Labrador, especially the people of the coast and the trappers. Judson Blake took a radio to his trapping ground and when he got messages he passed them on to the trappers. After a while my brother John Blake took a radio further up the river and passed the messages on to the upper trappers. The trappers went away much happier in the fall because they knew they would hear from their families. We were all happy. We had been cut off from the outside world.

Judson Blake wrote this letter to Dr. Burry while he was in his tilt on the trapline:

> *Gull Island*
> *Grand River, Labrador*

Dear Mr. Burry,

Just a note to let you know how I am hearing you. The first time I heard you speak to us on 80 meters. I tell you that I didn't touch that beaver until after I heard you. Then again to-night I turned on the radio and the choir at home was singing "I do not ask, O Lord." Well, Mr. Burry, I can't tell you how good it was to hear them. It was coming in clear as a bell. I wish I could thank the choir for all the trouble they are going to for us—and you also, Mr. Burry. I think that you people at home do not realize how much good this is doing us. It is appreciated by all. Everything I hear I send it to the trappers above me and also to the ones below.

Again I thank you very very much for what you are doing for us. I can go in the bush now in the morning feeling very happy.

I am your sincere friend.

> *Judson Blake*

The people of Labrador will never forget Dr. Burry. He served North West River, Mud Lake and Cartwright, travelling by dog team in winter and on the ship *Glad Tidings* in summer. Dr. Burry's boat and Dr. Paddon's Grenfell Mission boat gave a lot of service to the people of Labrador. We felt they understood what we had to go through and we thought a lot of them. They will never be forgotten in the old life of Labrador.

Rigolet families gathered to hear a visiting clergyman, 1877.

Elizabeth Goudie's maternal great-grandparents, Mersai Michella and Hannah, née Brooks, date unknown.

Elizabeth Goudie, née Blake, age sixteen, taken at Sebaskachu, 1918.

Henry Blake, Donald Baikie and Jim Goudie, wearing "dickies," taken at North West River, 1918.

Elizabeth Goudie's father's house at Mud Lake, 1922.

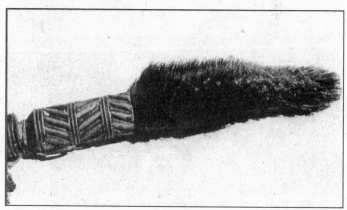

Elizabeth Goudie's porcupine quill brush. It was made by a Labrador settler and used to clean hairbrushes and combs.

Elizabeth Goudie with Robert Bruce and Horace, at Upitik (Merrifield) Bay in 1927—taken by an American doctor who was travelling with the explorer, Donald MacMillan. The doctor treated Bruce for his burns.

Jim Goudie, 1936, on his way to trapping grounds up Kenamu River. He is towing about two months' supplies on a homemade toboggan.

Reverend Lester Burry at work on a ham radio set he built to keep in touch with the trappers in the bush, 1937.

Trappers listening to Reverend Burry's broadcast.

Reverend Lester Burry, Joseph Blake (father of Elizabeth Goudie), Douglas Best, James Goudie (her husband) and Carl Hope—on board Glad Tidings II *at Mud Lake, 1938.*

The United Church and Reverend Burry's boat Glad Tidings II *at Mud Lake. Photo by Reverend Burry, 1930–40.*

Mud Lake, Labrador. Goudie family (left to right): Marie, May, Jim holding Chris, Elizabeth, Sergeant Carmen (baby unknown), Joe, Bill kneeling, 1943.

North Star School, Happy Valley, 1949—probably taken by teacher Betty Decker.

Reverend McKinny teaching Sunday School at Happy Valley, about 1950.

Preparing logs for construction of the United Church, Happy Valley, 1951.

Happy Valley circa 1950.

Mud Lake, Labrador. Standing (left to right): May Baikie, John Blake, Elizabeth Goudie; (sitting, left to right): Joseph Blake, Sarah Blake, circa 1950.

Jim Goudie.

Horace Goudie.

Bert Blake.

Mr. and Mrs. Goudie.

Elizabeth and Jim Goudie at home in Happy Valley, Labrador, August 1960.

Elizabeth Goudie's home, Happy Valley, Labrador.

The United Church at North West River, 1970.

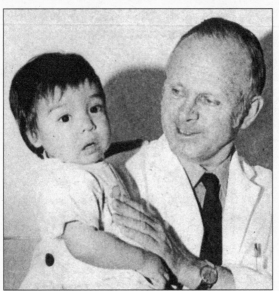

Dr. Tony Paddon (son of Dr. Harry Paddon) with an Eskimo patient at North West River Hospital, 1970.

Trapper Isaac Rich's tilt, 1971.

Inside trapper Isaac Rich's tilt, 1971.

Elizabeth Goudie.

Elizabeth Goudie speaks to school children at Goose Air Base, Goose Bay, Labrador, circa 1972–74.

Elizabeth Goudie receiving her honorary Doctor of Law degree at Memorial University of Newfoundland, Corner Brook, October 25, 1975. Dr. George Frecker, Chancellor of the university, presiding.

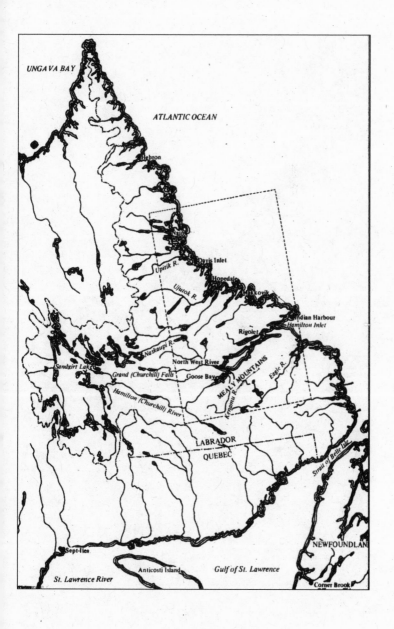

UNGAVA BAY

ATLANTIC OCEAN

Hebron

Upitik R.

Davis Inlet

Nain

Hopedale

Ujutok R.

Makkovik

Natkaupi R.

Indian Harbour
Hamilton Inlet

Rigolet

Sandgirt Lake

North West River

Grand (Churchill) Falls

Goose Bay

MEALY MOUNTAINS

Eagle R.

Kenamu R.

Hamilton (Churchill) River

LABRADOR

QUEBEC

Strait of Belle Isle

NEWFOUNDLAN

Sept-Iles

Anticosti Island

Gulf of St. Lawrence

St. Lawrence River

Corner Brook

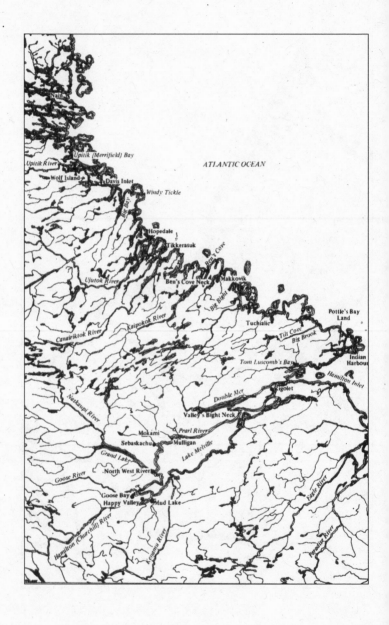

Nain

Upitik (Merrifield) Bay

Upitik River

Wolf Island

Davis Inlet

ATLANTIC OCEAN

Windy Tickle

Big Bay

Hopedale

Tikkerasuk

Rich's Cove

Ujutok River

Ben's Cove Neck

Makkovik

Big Bight

Canairiktok River

Kaipokok River

Tuchialic

Pottle's Bay Land

Till Cove

Big Brook

Naskaupi River

Tom Luscomb's Bay

Indian Harbour

Hamilton Inlet

Double Mer

Rigolet

Valley's Bight Neck

Mokami

Pearl River

Sebaskachu

Mulligan

Grand Lake

Lake Melville

Goose River

North West River

Eagle River

Goose Bay

Happy Valley

Mud Lake

Hamilton (Churchill) River

Kenamu River

Paradise River

III
A NEW LIFE FOR LABRADORIANS

They can search all over Canada,
*   such power they'll never find,*
As they found up in Labrador,
*   the mighty Churchill lying*
Be proud the natives of this land,
*   you've answered your country's call.*
You've done your share,
*   you gave to the the mighty Churchill Falls*

—from a song by Byron Chaulk

1. World War II and the Goose Bay Airport

1939 brought the old life of Labrador to a close. The war was on then and in 1940 people began to talk about an air base being built in Goose Bay. We were still living in Mud Lake. Jim and Horace were both trapping. In 1941 we saw two or three airplanes flying over Goose Bay and in the fall we got the news in Mud Lake that they were going to build an airport. In 1942 they started over where the dock is now. Everyone was so happy. There was going to be work for our men. We were going to have a chance to earn a steady income.

Jim worked all winter that year. A road was pushed through to Henry's Point and over to the Hamilton River and the air base was being built at the same time. The women didn't know much about what was going on.

One day in April 1943 our men came home to Mud Lake in the afternoon. Their foremen gave them a half day off to bring their families up to the air base to see a movie. We went up by dog team. There was a logging camp at Henry's Point and a truck was waiting there for us. When I first saw the truck I didn't feel much like getting on board, but because some of my children were afraid, I had to be brave. Everyone got on and we started towards the air base. The road was rough but the driver took extra care.

When we got to the airport we didn't know what to

make of it all. It was a completely new change of life from what we were used to.

We reached the building where they had the show and some of the officers came out and took the children. We went in and they treated the children with chocolate bars and gum and they turned off the lights and turned on the show. When it came on we couldn't believe our own eyes and ears, hearing people talking and seeing them moving on the screen. I thought a lot about it all after I got home that night.

We still lived on in Mud Lake. Jim worked in summer and trapped in winter. We were bothered with heavy colds and flu and a lot of us got quite sick. The doctor said it was because of the new people that had moved into Labrador. I had a bad case of pneumonia and we had to call the doctor. He brought me some drugs and I got better after a while. There were a few of our old people who died of heavy colds and pneumonia when the base first came to Goose Bay. After the base on the Canadian side was built up they got doctors and nurses in but we didn't see them because we had our own doctor in North West River—Dr. Paddon.

The war was still on then and there were soldiers on guard everywhere. No women or children were allowed on the base but we got to know one of the army officers, Sergeant Carmen. He often came to Mud Lake trout fishing and he would pay us a visit and have a cup of tea. He was very fond of the children.

Pneumonia in the family

One day in April my little boy Joe got very sick. He was running a high temperature and was sick for a long time and Dr. Paddon was away. I didn't know what to do as he was getting worse and I had nothing to treat him with. I

remembered a plant my mother used when we were growing up and I put my snowshoes on and went out and dug
some out of the snow. Mother called it "favour tea." It
grew very low on the ground. I took it home and boiled it.
Joe couldn't eat and I had an awful job to get him to take
the tea. It took me half an hour to get half a cupful into
him with a teaspoon. Two weeks later Sergeant Carmen
came over to the house from the base. Joe was still very
sick. He was not eating very well and was losing a lot of
weight. The sergeant went back to the base and got the
doctor for me. The doctor said Joe had a very bad attack
of pneumonia. He said there was nothing he could do at
the moment, but told me that if Joe started to vomit pus
to let him know right away.

About a week later I took Joe breakfast in the morning
and he started to vomit pus so I sent for the doctor. He
came over about eleven o'clock that night. When he saw
Joe he said he was very ill and asked Jim if we could leave
for the base right away. It was a very stormy night with a
heavy fall of snow. We had a small team of dogs. We started
back to the air base at one o'clock in the morning. We had
to go eight miles and the going underfoot was bad. The
doctor walked ahead of the dogs and Jim hauled on a line
with the dogs. Sergeant Carmen pushed behind on the
riding box that my little boy and I were in. We kept going
all night. The doctor had a jeep at the logging camp on the
south side of the Hamilton River. We didn't reach it until
six o'clock in the morning and my little boy cried every
time the *kamutik* hit a bump. Sergeant Carmen would
breathe a prayer, he was so uneasy about Joe. Jim and I
were very worried too.

We got Joe to the hospital about nine in the morning
and they took him right away for X-rays. He was gone an

hour. We were waiting for a doctor or a nurse to come and let us know what they had to do. While we were waiting Sergeant Carmen came along with the jeep and asked us if we were ready to go back to where the dogs were. Jim said we'd better go because the other children were home alone. Shortly after we left the doctor came looking for us. He had to operate right away and he wanted us to sign for the operation. Our oldest daughter Marie was working in the laundry and they found her and she signed for the operation. They told her it was only a fifty-fifty chance Joe would pull through because he was so weak. Marie said she was sure if there was a chance of saving Joe's life we would sign for the operation.

All that went on and we knew nothing about it until three days later when Sergeant Carmen came over to let us know. It was on a Sunday. We got ready and went up to the base to see Joe but he was too weak to talk to us. We stayed awhile with him but had to get home to the rest of the family. When I left I didn't have much hope for Joe. But when we went back again the following Sunday he was much better. The doctor told us he was over the worst of it. He said he would keep Joe there until he was fully recovered. He was there one month and it didn't cost us anything. We were very thankful we got him there in time. Sergeant Carmen had been a great help to us.

Shortly after he was transferred overseas and a couple of years later I heard he died of TB. We felt so sorry because he was a very kind man. I believe that it was through his help that our boy Joe is alive. When Joe came home from the hospital he was well and he grew up to be a healthy man.

Jim finds a downed plane

In 1943 Jim went trapping the latter part of February and a very cold snap of weather struck the day after he left. The night he got to the top of the hill to the second tilt, the temperature reached fifty below zero. He had to go out to one of his beaver traps in the morning. That night and plane crashed near the traps but he didn't know it as he had no radio. Goose Airport had been in touch with the plane and the last they heard it was about a hundred miles out, flying across the Mealy Mountains with the engines icing up. The pilot reported to Goose Bay that he didn't think he would make it over the hills. But when the plane came down it was only thirteen miles from Goose Bay in a straight line.

Jim went out in the morning to check his beaver trap and when he stooped down to shovel it out he thought he heard someone chop a stick of wood. He said to himself there couldn't be anyone there. There was no one who came that way, not even Indians. It was a very cold morning and he was in a hurry. He went on working at his trap. He heard another chop so he stopped and listened then and he heard someone throw down a stick of wood. Up the hill to the south there was a small pond but the top points of trees just about cut it off from sight. He couldn't see anything but he was sure then there was someone there. He started to walk toward the sounds and when he reached the pond he saw the airplane. Jim walked up to it and saw a man trying to make a fire. He spoke to the man, startling him. There had been seven men altogether. One was killed when the plane came down and one had a broken collar bone. The other five were all right. They had no snowshoes and were trying to make some out of parachute lines. They had lost their radio in the crash so couldn't contact Goose Bay.

Jim got a lot of dry wood for them and built a big fire. They placed the injured man near the fire where he could keep warm and Jim told them he would go for help. He left them around eleven in the morning and told them he would get to Mud Lake about eight that night and to Goose Air Base the next morning. He was worried about them. It was so cold he got enough dry wood for them for a night and a day and told them not to leave the airplane. He had his supper when he reached home at eight and went to bed. He was up again at three to start for Goose Bay. It was about eight miles. He managed to get a truck at Henry's Point and reached the air base early in the morning. Soon after he told the news to headquarters a message came in from one of the search planes that they had sighted the crash. The commanding officer sent another plane out and Jim went with them, but when they landed on the pond they got bogged down in water and snow and couldn't take off. They had to build camp and food was dropped to them. Jim took the man with the broken collar bone to his tilt and looked after him.

A few days later, Jim got sick and was sick for three or four days. In the meantime the air force hired three dog teams from Mud Lake and managed to reach the top of the hill. It was nine days before they got everyone out. The dog teams got the wounded man out to Goose Bay. Everything turned out all right but they were lucky. Jim said they would have perished if he hadn't happened to find them. They had intended to try to walk out but it would have been a twenty-mile walk.

When Jim was sick the pilot looked after him. He told Jim that when his plane came down one wing tore off in the trees. He and the co-pilot were sitting in the open air when the nose came off but they weren't hurt. Jim used to

get letters from them a long while after they went back to
Canada. They never forgot Jim for saving their lives.

It was the first of March before everything was straightened out. Jim didn't get paid in cash for it but they gave
us some food and that was just as good.

The move to Happy Valley

That was our last year living in Mud Lake. The next year,
1944, we moved to the Valley. I had lived twenty-five years
in Mud Lake. I was sorry to move because I had gardens
in Mud Lake.

2. A New Life in Happy Valley

When we came to live here in Happy Valley there were no roads or anything like that. The men had to cross in boat or canoe and walk to Henry's Point to go to work in the morning. It was not called Happy Valley then. There were only a few families there—about nine on the mainland and about three on Birch Island.

We came in August and had to cut all the birches and spruces off the bank to put down our tent camp. Although my husband was working every day, he got some second-hand lumber and whatever else he could get to build a little shack for the winter. We camped from August until October when we moved into the house. It was pretty small, about eighteen by twenty feet, and we also had my oldest daughter and her husband with us for the winter. Marie had been married in June 1944.

House building

The first part of the summer we had to fetch water over the bank. As soon as Jim started to lay the foundation of the house, he put in a pump. We had the pump down a twenty-two foot pipe so we had beautiful water then.

At first we had to go to the base for all our groceries. When the days got warm in the spring, Jim and I would leave the house very early in the morning and walk over to Henry's Point. There we got aboard a truck going to the base. After a while the Hudson's Bay had a store at the base and then we could get through on the Hudson's Bay truck, but the women had it pretty tough at first, having to ride in open trucks.

The early settlers had to go to North West River for their groceries. They went in the fall and again in the winter by dog team.

After the road was put in and people were building all along it on both sides, the air force measured out this side of the road and I believe the other side of the Hamilton River Road and they gave us a plot 100 feet by 300 feet. The houses were built to be sufficient for our families. Jim built ours according to the air force rule—seventy-five square feet per person—and we had a number of children home at the time. So we ended up with a big house.

Schooling

We had three boys and two girls at home. We found out after we moved up here that a lady named Alice Perrault was starting school in her house. There were ten or twelve children of school age here then. She took two of my boys into her school, Bill and Joe. Chris was too small and our youngest girl went to work at the US Army Base in the girls' barracks. I kept the other one home.

It wasn't too long before Mrs. Perrault couldn't get all the children in her living room and kitchen. People were moving in so fast that she had to see about getting another school. The people got together and presented the school problem to the commanding officer at Goose Air Base and after a while they gave us an old building. It was quite large and Mrs. Perrault went on teaching school there. She had to get some help so they contacted the Newfoundland Government who sent a couple of teachers.

Trip to hospital in St. John's, Newfoundland

Meanwhile the boys continued to stay in school and Jim was still building our house. Shortly after baby James was born in September 1947 I had an abscess in my breast and it got so bad I had to go to the American Hospital and have it drained. While I was in hospital they discovered I had some other troubles with my health and wanted me to go to St. John's for an operation. They said I couldn't go on the way I was. They didn't have the instruments there to do it or they would have while I was in the hospital. They said it would take about a month because my blood had to be built up. I was never in a hospital before for any kind of sickness. I never was very sick in my life until then. I didn't want to leave my three-month-old baby, but I got one of my daughters to look after him.

I left for St. John's in January 1948. Jim's blind brother Albert went out with me. He was going to an old people's home. It was our first time in an airplane and it was a freight plane. We had to drop off some freight at Seven Islands and going on to Harmen Air Base we struck a storm of heavy snow. When we got to Harmen Field it was hard landing. It was a very rough night.

An RCMP officer from Goose Bay came out with us. When we reached the USAF hospital he told the doctor he had a couple of patients from Labrador and he went on to his home. The nurse came to meet us and took us inside. She took me to the washroom and when I was getting ready I took down my hair. She said, "You have lovely hair," and I thanked her. "Oh," she said, "you can speak English," and I just laughed. I was tired and miserable from the trip.

She showed us to our ward and then left us. As she went out she turned a switch on the wall. I didn't notice what it was and went on to bed. The room got awfully cold. I had to get up and get some more blankets. Albert began to say he was cold. It was getting daylight then so the day nurse came on just after.

"Oh my," she said, "you people must be cold. You have no heat." She turned the heat on and shortly afterwards a man came in the little day room and asked us if we would like a cooked breakfast and I said I would. He just nodded his head to me and came in later with our breakfast. He never talked to us. He just set the tray down and went out and the old man said to me, "I wonder why they don't talk to us?" I said, "I don't know." About ten o'clock they brought in one of the padres to see us and he began trying to talk Eskimo to us. I said, "I don't understand," and he said, "What language do you speak?" Then I said, "English, the best I can." He asked where we came from and I told him Goose Bay. "Oh," he said, "we thought you came from Fort Chimo.[21] We turned the heat off last night because we thought you weren't used to it."

I began to realize they hadn't asked us anything when we came in. We didn't mind if they thought we came from Chimo, but I think it was ignorance on their part not to ask where we came from before they treated us that way. We did have a miserable night on account of it. After it was all over, Albert and I laughed about it. I said, "That goes to show how little the city people really know about Labrador and its people."

It was about thirty-six below zero. We were held up in the USAF hospital until Sunday evening because it was stormy. We went on to St. John's and it was very rough landing. We had help from a jeep to get up to the hangar.

It was getting late and I had to be taken to the General Hospital and Albert went on to the old people's home. When I reached the hospital I reported to the office and got to where I was going about twelve o'clock at night. I had to go through all the routines of checking into the ward with the head nurse.

I was taken to my bed and I could hear the patients speaking to each other quietly and I heard one say, "She's not from Newfoundland. She's a Protestant. I think she may be from England." I could have really laughed out loud. At Harmen Field they thought I was Eskimo and here they thought I was English. The whole trip was quite an experience for me.

At the hospital they discovered that I was very anemic and I had to have my blood built up. It took a month. They did the operation in the early part of February, and that day, Albert was burned. I was sitting in my bed waiting for my needles and the different things that had to be done and there were a lot of cars coming to and from the hospital. I didn't know what the meaning of it was, but three days later I discovered that was the day the old people's home burned and Albert was among those who died. They kept all newspapers and everything from me for three days. I wouldn't have got the news the third day but a newsboy came through and I bought a paper. I was disturbed about it all evening and the nurses didn't like it. I had been in a pretty weak condition when I arrived, so I stayed in the hospital until I was recovered enough to be moved out to the annex. I stayed for two more weeks before they thought I was strong enough to fly back to Goose Bay.

When I got back to Goose Bay I discovered my two youngest children were down with the measles and my granddaughter was so sick I had to get right to work and contact the doctors on the base and have her taken to the hospital. They said we just got her there in time, that she had pneumonia with the measles. So it was a long time before I got straightened out.

The years went by and I didn't bother to keep in touch very much with the Valley because I was sick most of the time and trying to keep my children in school, and Jim was busy building the house and the furniture while still working at the base. I was laid up so many years with heart trouble and operations and other problems that I couldn't keep up with things going on in Happy Valley.

Rev. McKinny

It wasn't long after people started moving in to Happy Valley that they wanted a minister. After a while, by calling meetings with the officials on the base and the government, we got a man to come and serve as a community minister. His name was Reverend McKinny and he had two daughters who took up teaching in the day school and Sunday school. It wasn't very long before the population outgrew that school. People were moving in so fast we couldn't keep up with it.

The first building that had been brought down from the air base to serve as a school was also used for church meetings and church services and after a while Rev. McKinny got the people started building a new church. Before the church was finished, other denominations wanted their own church. There were four denominations here then— the Church of England, Moravian, Pentecostal and United Church. The United people ended up with the church Rev. McKinny started. All the other people were busy getting ready to build their own churches but the school problem arose again.

This time the MacNamara Construction Company agreed to build a three-room school. Miss Betty Decker, our first principal, named it "North Star." But it was over-crowded in a couple of years.

The cry went out again for a bigger school. The United Church had a meeting and the men of the church made a pledge to raise so much money over a period of three years for a six-room school. We got it started and we got our school built and by that time there were a lot of Pentecostal children. The Church of England had been building a school too, so when both schools were opened up, we took in the Pentecostal children and the Church of England school took in the Moravian children. This all came about because of a teacher from the Moravian Mission, Mrs. Alice Perrault, who opened up two rooms in her first little shack. She used plywood for tables, one in her kitchen and one in her living room. She worked hard to see the schools open up. She and her husband also started Boy Scouts and Girl Guides.

The first hospital

Then we got our little hospital clinic. It only had five beds. Two little wards, one for expectant mothers and three beds in another ward. That was our first hospital.[22] Our first nurse was Miss Rhodes. She came out from England and when she started there were about five hundred people here. This little hospital was run by the Grenfell Mission. Our local doctor, Dr. Tony Paddon, was the head of it. He visited it twice a week and if there were emergencies he came up from the main hospital at North West River.

The mission had a little airplane they used for the coast and a snowmobile in winter so anyone needing an operation was taken to North West River by the little airplane or the snowmobile. The Canadian Air Force and the American Air Force helped out a great deal by taking emergencies in their hospitals. Dr. Tony Paddon also served the coast as far north as Nain and as far south as St. Anthony. So he was a very busy doctor. We all played a little part in building up Happy Valley.

Rev. Lester Burry was still with us then doing mission work for the United Church. But two or three years after Happy Valley was started he went back to St. John's to live.

The ten years between 1946 and 1956 were about the busiest, I believe, in the life of Happy Valley—the schools and churches and the little hospital and the people building their homes.

Bill, Joe, Chris and Jim (Junior) were born here in Happy Valley so these four sons got their schooling here. Bill took a course in auto mechanics. Joe got his Grade Eleven and he works with the CBC as an announcer. Christopher works in Churchill Falls and Jim joined the Royal Canadian Armed Forces. He got Grade Eleven there. Dad was very pleased that four of his sons got to school. He never had any schooling himself but he learned to read and write and he was very clever at mathematics. He could do all his own carpentry work, building boats and canoes and houses.

My first four children were brought up as trappers but they could do almost any work. Horace was a clever hunter and he learned carpentry. He made his own snowshoes and his sled and many other things he learned from experience, not books. My three girls learned also about cooking and making their own clothes. I taught them all that I knew about housekeeping and Jim did the best he could with Horace.

Through the fifties all our girls got married and left home and I was left with the boys. I was no better off then because I had to do all the work myself and I wasn't getting any younger. I found it pretty hard sometimes.

Our house was finished by then. It was a two-storey house with eleven rooms. Jim and I were so glad that we had it all paid for in the fall of 1958. Jim said to me, "We will be able to put some money by for ourselves when we grow older," and I was so happy because it was the first time in our life we could do that.

3. THE DEATH OF MY HUSBAND

All the boys were growing up and getting work. We still had one in school. He was eleven years old when in late December of 1958 my husband was brought home one day with a heart condition. He was very sick and we didn't know how bad it was. The report from the doctor said Jim would never work again. We didn't know what his trouble was and the American doctor sent for Dr. Paddon. He said there were broken tissues between the heart and lung. The doctors claimed Jim was too old for them to heal so we didn't know what we would have to expect then.

He suffered quite a lot with it the first year. The doctors gave him tests once every month and after a year was up he was no better. They told me there was no hope of him healing up but he might live four or five years if we would take good care of him and not let him work at all. The first year he was quite sick all the time but at the end of that year he seemed a little better. Then he got quite depressed and we didn't know what to do for him or what we could get for him to occupy his mind. We got a couple of rabbits and built a little yard and a house and he fed them every morning and evening. He was quite happy with this job and the little children would come around to see his rabbits and he enjoyed children.

In the spring the rabbits had young ones and he was really happy about that. The family felt better too to see him so happy. In summertime he was very good, but in winter he had to stay inside most of the time and I had to be responsible for running the home then. I was very busy sometimes and Jim would find the evening very long waiting for me to get my work done so I could sit and talk with him. He was growing blind fast too. The doctor could not do anything for his eyes. He had some kind of pressure at the back of his eyes that they couldn't help.

As the years went on he seemed to be more depressed and lonely. After four years the doctor told me the tissues had healed a little, so Jim could get about among the neighbours and he enjoyed that quite a lot. It was a terrible time. I always hoped he would get better. Jim had a birthday in November of 1962. He was seventy.

That Christmas he wanted to go and see his grandchildren. I was going to get a taxi but he wanted to walk there. It was not very far so we walked and he spent the afternoon with the children trying out their toys and he had a game of cards with the girls and their husbands. He was happy and enjoyed himself.

He kept quite well until January 4. He got up that day and had his breakfast about ten o'clock. I was busy getting ready to do my laundry and he told me that if I would wait he would pump the water for me. I always tried to keep him from doing work like that. He insisted on helping me so I let him pump those buckets for me. Then he went and sat down and I looked at him and he didn't look well. I watched for about five minutes and I asked him if he didn't feel well. He said he had that pain again so I sat by him and I noticed the colour was changing about his ears. I asked him if he wanted me to call the nurse and he said yes. He said call the family too, so I called my son into the house. We called a taxi and got him to the hospital and the doctor saw him right away and while the doctor was seeing to him I went out and called the family. I rushed back into the hospital again and three of the boys got there and two of the girls and I said a few words to him. The doctors agreed to take him to North West River hospital because there was no room for him in the little hospital clinic we had at Happy Valley. I said to him, "I will be coming with you to look after you." "That will be good," he said, and I heard him make a noise and I looked around at him and he was dying. He passed out of this world five minutes later, about twelve o'clock in 1963, the fourth of January.

He was seventy years old. We were married forty-two years. They were good years. He was an easy man to live with, good-natured and very dedicated to his family and me. He was a very hard worker. He never went to school in his life but he learned to read and he could look after his own affairs. He loved to read. He could build anything. He had a good home built for us when he died and it was all paid for. I was very happy that I could live in my own home. He was the father of ten children—six boys and four girls—and the grandfather of thirty-two grand-children when he died.

He was a trapper all his life until a few years before he died when he worked with the Americans as a packer and crater in No. 2 Warehouse at Goose Bay. He trapped a lot of land in this part of Labrador. He trapped on the Hamilton River and to the height of land on Sandgirt Lake. He trapped to the north Kaipokok River and Ujutok and the head of Grand Lake in back of Naskaupi River. He did a lot of travelling in his day. It was a great loss to the family when he died. He was a very patient man liked by most everyone and he was known in this part of Labrador as Uncle Jim Goudie. He could play the mouth organ. That was his pastime when he was trapping, mostly on Sunday. He never worked on Sunday unless he had to. He kept that day for rest.

Our family missed him very much and I carried on alone then without him. It's seven years now since he has been gone and I am looking after the place and running things myself. I keep boarders to help myself so life hasn't been easy for me either. All my family are married and gone now but two boys. One stays at home and the other one is in the Armed Forces. When I think of Jim and his family, I look back over the years and recall the times when he would come home from his trapping lines half-starved and frost-bitten. He walked 300 miles when he trapped the height of land near the Quebec border. He travelled miles inside the Churchill Falls when we lived in Mud Lake. When I think of all the hardships he went through for us it brings tears to my eyes so I keep my house open for his children to come and go as they like. I know he would want that so it is going to be that way as long as I can keep it open. We worked side by side those forty-two years together, and it was pretty rough sometimes. We respected each other and when he was taken from me I didn't feel too bad. Life is meant to be that way. I think a person has nothing to regret when they are happy and we were very happy, so I am quite content now. There is always something to do and always something to think about.

4. PRESENT LIFE

Recently I was invited to speak on Labrador to the Grade Five class at Hamilton High School and I also was invited to the Robert Leckie High School in Spruce Park to speak to a Grade Nine class. I was a bit worried because I was afraid they would ask questions I couldn't answer, but I talked to them for half an hour and they didn't ask many questions. They just listened and I could see by their faces they didn't know very much about Labrador and its life. I was very glad I spoke to them because they seemed to enjoy it so much. I was also invited out to a Grade Eight class. They served us lunch and I stayed awhile at their dance. It makes me very happy that our children have such a chance. I hope they will learn to be thankful. I guess I get carried away when I am in the classroom and I see all the nice things they have to work with. I thought back over the years about myself and the things I had learned with my brain and my hands. I could do anything from embroidery work to chopping wood without a book, but I was happy and thankful I had a healthy body to do it with. We live differently now and I hope it's for the best. I hope we will soon have peace on earth where everybody can enjoy themselves and it's up to us to do our best to bring it about.

Trip to Montreal

I have been able to go places a little since my husband passed on. I have been to St. John's and to Corner Brook and Grand Falls. Once I was appointed by the church to go to a conference. It was quite a change for me and I really enjoyed it. Then in 1967 I took a month's holiday with my friend Marion Leith. She was working with the 4-H Branch in Newfoundland and I met her during a trip she made to Labrador. So when she took her holiday to Montreal in October of '67 she invited me to come along with her and another friend from North West River. Marion was already in Montreal and had a room for us, so we left Goose Bay and joined her. I had never been in a big city before. We arrived at six o'clock in the morning and it was raining and the air was hard to breathe. I had left Labrador breathing fresh air and landed in the city and it was just too much for me. When we got up after trying to have a rest Marion decided to try to get another room further out of the city. We moved that same day and by the end of it I was just exhausted.

I was trying to fight my nerves. I never dreamed a city could be so full of traffic and people. We got a nice, quiet place for the night but after I got to bed I was sick to my stomach. It was just too much for me. So the girls went out to Expo in the morning and I stayed in my room all day. I went out for lunch in the evening to a little restaurant. I still felt all in a daze but I was feeling a little better so I went back to my room and waited for the girls. When they got back about eleven o'clock that night they said to me, "Will you be able to go tomorrow?" and I said I would try. We had a nice room and the people were kind, so in the morning we walked to a restaurant for our breakfast and it was nice, crisp morning air. I enjoyed my walk. I was feeling very good but I was not sure I was going to hold out all day. But I was going to make a very hard try.

After breakfast we took the bus and went to the Expo site and when we got there the people were going in all directions like a pack of flies. I didn't want the girls to know I was a bit nervous. Every now and then they would check on me to see if I was all right so I managed to keep up with them. We had to go or be walked over. When we got to the revolving steps they showed me how to step on and off. I said to myself if I fall down here I will never get up because no one will see and I will be walked over. I felt like screaming with fear sometimes. That was the first day.

The second day I knew a little more about it so I tried to ignore all the people that passed before me and to mind my own business. The second day it was better. I went to Expo every day for nine days. I got inside a number of pavilions. I enjoyed the food and all the flowers. That was the first time I saw a city but I wouldn't like to live in the city. I came back in ten days to Goose Bay.

Trip to Toronto

I was looking after a small baby for one of the teachers that winter. My plans were made for another trip early in the summer so I got ten days off in 1968. I got an invitation from the United Church Women to go to Toronto but I didn't mind going there because I knew the minister, Rev. Sellers. He had once been stationed in Happy Valley. I arrived in Toronto on Good Friday. Sunday night Mrs. William Sealy Mercer came to visit. Her husband served Labrador for several years and had married us in 1920. He left Labrador in 1921 and went to Flowers Cove on Newfoundland Island. In 1924 he got caught out in a winter's storm and perished. Mrs. Denzil Rideout came to see me too because her husband was interested in the church in Labrador. He was the one who turned the sod for our little church in Mud Lake in 1938.

The rest of my time in Toronto was spent sightseeing and talking to groups of United Church women about Labrador. I reached home safely and I was very glad to be back in Labrador again. The city didn't appeal to me as a place I would like to live.

Churchill Falls

1971 seems a special year in the history of my life. I made a trip to Churchill Falls in the latter part of the month of May. I spent two weeks in Twin Falls and a night at Churchill where my son Chris and I took a drive around the campsite. We passed Sona Lake where my husband's brother Fred Goudie trapped. I was also at Unknown River where Arch Goudie trapped but couldn't get to where Jim trapped at Lobstick Lake. The road was too rough to travel on at that time, but I saw the land and it thrilled my heart even to see it and to be able to visit that land where all the oldtime trappers trapped. My son Horace trapped there.

I didn't see Churchill Falls because they were busy working laying cables and it was out of bounds to visitors. I never saw Churchill Falls in their natural form and I never will now because they are gone. My son Chris told me a person can walk across the falls with only his boots on. It's hard to believe such a project could come in my lifetime. I stood there looking all around me with tears in my eyes thinking back to the old days when there were only Indians and a few trappers. We were standing beside Fred Goudie's trapping place at Sona Lake which he named after his daughter. I was looking at the hills out in the distance where Jim trapped and now it is all flooded with water. It will never be seen anymore.

Hubbard Expedition recalled

I was listening to the CBC one day and they were telling the story of Leonidas Hubbard and Dillon Wallace who started to make a trip across to Ungava Bay in 1903. They took the wrong river. We were told it was the fault of their map. They got so far and found out they were going wrong and tried to get back but they were very far out with food supply almost gone. Mr. Hubbard gave out and couldn't travel so he told the guide to go on and try to get Dillon Wallace out if he could. They knew Hubbard would be dead if they ever got back. They went on but just before they got back to Grand Lake Mr. Wallace collapsed. He told the guide to go on and he would try to keep alive until he could get help. All he had to eat then was a piece of skin from a caribou they killed on their way in. The guide was George Elson. He reached North West River and another party started right back. The party that went back was Allen Goudie, Duncan McLean, Donald Blake and Gilbert Blake. When they reached Dillon Wallace he was still alive so they stayed with him until he was able to walk and while they were waiting a couple of the men went on and found the body of Mr. Hubbard. I believe it was the month of November 1903.

In 1904 Mrs. Hubbard came to Labrador to try to finish her husband's trip and to put a monument where he lost his life. She chose a party from around North West River and Gilbert Blake was one of them. He was only fifteen years old then. Gilbert Blake was my father's half-brother and Allen Goudie was my husband's brother. Gilbert Blake is still alive. He is in his eighties now and is losing his hearing and eyesight.

Recently I went to see Uncle Bert Blake. He couldn't tell me much about it but he had a copy of *The Beaver* magazine published in 1960 by the Hudson's Bay Company, with pictures and a short story of Mrs. Hubbard's trip across Labrador from the head of Grand Lake to Ungava.[23] Mrs. Hubbard made the trip with George Elson, two Cree trappers and Gilbert Blake, my uncle, who is like a Montagnais Indian, although there is no Montagnais blood in him. English is the white blood and maybe Eskimo from the Labrador side. He and his wife had a big family. She was about two-thirds Scottish—a McLean before she married him. He named his first daughter Mira Benson after Mrs. Hubbard. Uncle Bert's wife has a vegetable garden in summer. They live on Hamilton River Road in Happy Valley. There are very few old people left now that were born in the tail eighties. They are almost all gone and when I see one of the old-timers go it hurts me very deeply because I say to myself, "Another old trapper gone."

First trappers to hunt Grand (Churchill) Falls

Uncle Bert also told me the story about himself and four other trappers who were hunting inside the Grand Falls, the name of Churchill Falls in those days.

"You know," he said, "William Montague, Henry Groves, Charlie Goudie, Arch Goudie and I were the first white men who went in there to trap among the Indians in the early 1900s; they didn't like it. They tried to drive us out every way. But," he said, "we were young men then and we didn't care, we stuck it out all winter. We trapped from the fall in November and were still trapping up to the first of February when we were running low on food and provisions, grub. Charles Goudie and Henry Groves decided to come to North West River to fetch some more food and Arch Goudie and myself were left in there with William Montague. We all had our own separate trapping lines so Arch went out on his line, struck up his traps, and we were going down in the valley of the river to wait for the boys, because we only had a little food. We were taking off for a little while till they got back with food. "Arch Goudie had just struck up his lines when six Indians came out one afternoon. They were so cross about us stealing their trapping. They had gone to Seven Islands and came back again after the winter. There were six men and they were so mad that one man took his gun and held it to Arch's head while the others robbed away all his grub and burned down his tilt. I came there a little while after and I didn't know this happened, so there we were left without food, only a little bit I had.

"We talked about it and decided we would try to get back to the valley below the Grand Falls and try and find some more food because there were trappers right up as far as the Hill Portage. We knew there were trappers there and that they would have gone home but we hoped there would be some food left, so we started out. We got to the valley of the river, after being four days and a half without any food at all, and made the first tilt. We opened the door and looked in and there were two bags of flour all ripped open and the flour gone. I said to Arch, 'Boy, we're finished. We'll just stay here and die in the tilt where the others will find us because Charlie and Henry are not due back yet for a couple of weeks.' I thought we'd just stay there and starve because we couldn't do anything about it anyway; there was nowhere else to go. We went to make a fire in the stove and there was a box quite close to the stove and it didn't look to be a very important box, but we pulled it away because we thought it was going to catch fire. We went to pull it away and it was heavy, and when we opened it up there was flour and tea and everything inside and it saved our lives."

Uncle Bert said the Indians were really nasty then. They didn't like white men coming onto their land. They counted their land from Grand Falls to Seven Islands and they wanted no white men on it. This is how they treated the first white men in there.

IV
YESTERDAY AND TOMORROW

*They can talk of their cities, their riches
  untold,
All the things that they bought with their
  silver and gold,
All the gold that they have couldn't buy
  what I see,
From high on the mountain of old
  Mokami.*

—from a song by Byron Chaulk

1. What Life Has Meant

When I think of the life of today compared to fifty years ago I find it pretty hard to express an opinion of the changes to one's peace of mind and contented heart. I would rather live back fifty years ago, because today you turn on your radio or television and you hear all sorts of news about going to the moon or war or whatever and you feel afraid that something fearful is going to happen. I think the years have brought many good things and also bad things. I think the people of Labrador were not prepared for such changes in such a short time. They did not know how to cope with them. It was something new to them and they did not stop to think of what they would have to face later as the result of their young people having the opportunity to get an education.

I have been here about twenty years and I have seen the changes that have taken place. I don't know much about the clubs or Bingo or anything like that because that doesn't draw my attention. I have a family of my own. A part of them grew up here. A part of them grew up in the old life of Labrador. I have suffered more sorrows with the latter part of my family than I did with the first four who were born before the base was stationed here. I think if parents don't take time to love and serve their children as they ought, there are sorrows ahead as well as joys.

One thing I am glad of is that my children don't have to work as hard as we did. Money has been very plentiful compared to what we had in the past. It has done a lot of good for this town. It brought our churches, our schools and our little hospital which has proved a good service to this town. Our nurses have worked very hard and have served us well. Many little children have had lots of milk and good food and clothing which the children of the past did not have. I have looked at the nice clothing and thought back to my own little ones. How proud I would have been if only I could have had some of these good things for my little ones.

My last four children had a lot more to eat and wear than the first four. They had milk and fruit and many things. But my first four seem to be happier than the last four with all they got. They have a lot and they still want more. They will never know how hard their first brothers and sisters had it, though they were happy with the little they had.

If I had to live my life over again I would still choose the trapper's life. It was a good life, believe me, and now I am trying to live a different life and trying to keep up with the times of today. I try not to be too far behind. I will never keep with it all and I don't think I will try. Things are a lot easier now and I am thankful for that. I have an electric washer and an iron. I used my hands all my life until Joe got to work and bought me a washer. Jim had all he could do to build the house and pay all the bills.

I am still quite active and enjoying life. I am so happy to see spring again. I love the little birds and to see the green coming forth and I have my eyesight to enjoy it and I am not crippled so I may be good for another ten years.

I would like to live to see this writing of our life and the life of the Labrador trappers published. These people all knew each other and were always happy to get together. We would be out at the door to greet any trappers who passed by and invite them in to have a cup of tea. Sometimes they stayed for tea and if it was getting late and they had to travel on we would at least hear a bit of news from elsewhere. We would be very happy if someone would stay for a night because we would hear of all the happenings, good or not so good. We would enjoy that very much.

It was a good life, a very plain life. Just poor people—most of us were alike, but life didn't seem hard. We were honest with each other and if you had two meals of meat and your neighbour had none you shared with him. I believe the burdens we had to bear were made easier because we shared with each other.

The house I have now I call the house of my prayers because when my children were small and I didn't have enough room for them I used to pray for a bigger house someday. But now they are all gone on their own and I am by myself. I had a bedtime song I used to sing to them when I was putting them to bed. When my husband was away and we were left alone they would be asking for their daddy—when would he come home? I would sing this little song that I made up:

> *Hush my dear, lie still and slumber,*
> *Holy angel guard thy bed;*
> *Heavenly blessings without number, gently falling on*
> *thy head.*

I sang this song with the baby in my arms, someone else trying to get there, and someone wanting a piece of bread. Now when I think back over the years I wonder how I managed.

2. Looking Forward

I hope the people of Labrador will take a stand for themselves, for there is no excuse now that they have a chance to get an education.

I am very proud of my country Labrador. That name goes very deep within my being, the beauty of its rivers and lakes and the beautiful green forests and the hills and the great white Mealy Mountains.

I look out over the miles and miles of hillside untouched by man and I wonder how much longer are we going to be able to keep its beauty. The name Labrador holds something hard to explain but I would like to explain it in my own way, and that is peace—a deep peace within that helps to make all its hard work easier to take. I really believe this within myself and most of the old-timers I talk to feel the same way. They say we will never have the same kind of peace anymore, but I hope our young people will pick up where we left off and try to keep peace and be proud of this great land.

Now the days of the trappers are behind us but I am proud I had the chance to live such a life. The wife of a trapper played a great part in it because she had to live as a man five months of the year. She had to use her gun and she had to know how to set nets to catch fish and also how to judge the right distance from the shore to cut her fish holes because if you cut them in too shoal[24] water you would have to move out into deeper water and then you would have to cut another hole in three-and-a-half feet of ice. I learned all of this the hard way. That was the outdoors life. Indoors if you were a mother you had to know how to look after your children, you had to cook, make clothes for the family, sealskin boots, and often you had to act as a doctor or nurse and I am not ashamed of it because that kind of life fit our country at that time. There was no other way out. I will go anywhere and be proud to talk about it.

Now things are changed, even the name of Grand River to Churchill River. Many of us didn't like it when we heard of the change because Grand River was its name since the 1800s and to the trappers it was their home and I would say their birthright. I have nothing against the name Churchill—he was a good man too—but no one asked us if we were satisfied having it changed. If Joe Smallwood had seen the trappers return from Grand River with their frostbitten faces, half-starved and exhausted, he might have thought twice before he changed it, but that is beside the point now. For many old-timers it still is Grand River, but for the younger generation it will be Churchill River and I hope they will treat it with respect. I hope the younger people will take pride in Labrador because it's a country of beauty and wealth. Its people were a *people* in the past. The trappers made their own laws, they respected each other's laws and they carried them out to the best of their ability. I will never change deep within my heart and I hope I can be a friend to people. We should all strive to live in peace with one another. That's the only way to live right.

Epilogue

Elizabeth Goudie was awarded an honorary Doctor of Law degree at the 1975 Fall Convocation of Memorial University of Newfounland, Corner Brook, to recognize her contribution to the recorded history of Labrador and a lifetime of achievement.

Her elder son Horace Goudie followed her example, publishing a book titled *Trails to Remember* in 1992.

Much of the revenue from the sale of her autobiography *Woman of Labrador* was donated by Elizabeth Goudie to the Paddon Memorial Senior Citizens Home located in Happy Valley, Labrador. It was in a room which she furnished that she passed peacefully away in her sleep the night of June 10, 1982, at eighty years of age.

She had requested that her daughters prepare her body for burial, in a casket made by her sons and one grandson and the funeral service was to take place in the back yard of her home at 123 Hamilton River Road. It was attended by a large number of friends and relatives on a warm, sunny Labrador day. Among those present was the Premier of the province, A. Brian Peckford, and his Cabinet Ministers, one of whom was her son Joe.

The music of several Labrador musicians and the words of her friends and family were an appropriate setting in which to send her on her well-earned way.

Joe Goudie

ENDNOTES

1 The name Michella was later changed to Michelin.
2 Newfoundland and Labrador did not become a province until 1949.
3 A London-based health organization started in the late 1800s for the benefit of poor fishermen along the Labrador coast and parts of northern Newfoundland.
4 Older respected people were generally called Aunt or Uncle whether they were relatives or not.
5 Name of Grenfell Mission's boat.
6 Freeman Saunders was his father.
7 Actually Lake Melville.
8 Also called Labrador Tea.
9 Groups of ducks, geese, birds and seals are called companies by the settlers.
10 The term "liveyer" (contraction of "live here") distinguished the settlers from the more transient summer fishermen who were called either "stationers" (they had a summer house on the coast of Labrador) or "floaters" (they lived on board their ships). The term is supposed to have originated as the reply to the question: Where do you live?
11 Dog-sled.
12 A dickie is a one-piece pullover parka with fur around the hood.
13 A coach- or riding box about six feet long. It was put on the *kamutik* to protect the woman and children from the cold.
14 Mrs. Goudie's occasional use of present tense indicates the tremendous impact many events and times had on her.
15 Infection of the uterus of a woman who has recently given birth—puerperal metritis.
16 To check for caught seals and to repair any rips.
17 Toboggan.
18 Length of tree a man could carry on his shoulders—usually ten to twelve feet long.
19 Montagnais-Naskapi Indian word used by settlers to denote a feast or party. The Indians use the word to describe a special religious ritual that involves the eating of bone marrow and fat from the caribou.

20 Denzil Rideout was a United Church official who came to Mud Lake in 1938 for the church corner-stone ceremony.
21 An Eskimo community in Ungava Bay on the north shore of Quebec.
22 Nursing station.
23 Alan Cooke, "A Woman's Way," *The Beaver,* Summer 1960, Outfit 291 pp. 40–45.
24 Shallow.